ARE YOU LGBTQ?

Jeanne Nagle

BISEXUAL

ACCEPTANCE

TRANSGENDER

GAY

LESBIAN

IDENTITY

Enslow Publishing
101 W. 23rd Street
Suite 240
New York, NY 10011
USA

enslow.com

GOT
ISSUES?

Published in 2016 by Enslow Publishing, LLC.
101 W. 23rd Street, Suite 240, New York, NY 10011

Library of Congress Cataloging-in-Publication Data

Names: Nagle, Jeanne.
Title: Are you LGBTQ? / Jeanne Nagle.
Description: New York : Enslow Publishing, 2016. | Series: Got Issues? | Includes index.
Identifiers: ISBN 9780766071391 (library bound)
Subjects: LCSH: Gay rights—United States—Juvenile literature. | Gay liberation movement—United
  States—Juvenile literature. |Homosexuality—United States—Juvenile literature.
Classification: LCC HQ76.26 N338 2016 | DDC 306.76'60835—dc23

Printed in the United States of America

To Our Readers: We have done our best to make sure all websites in this book were active and appropriate when we went to press. However, the author and the publisher have no control over and assume no liability for the material available on those websites or on any websites they may link to. Any comments or suggestions can be sent by e-mail to customerservice@enslow.com.

Portions of this book originally appeared in the book *Homosexuality.*

Disclaimer: For many of the images in this book, the people photographed are models. The depictions do not imply actual situations or events.

Contents

Orientation and Identification

It is funny, meaning odd, that something as deeply personal as people's love and sex lives has become such a hot topic of public debate. Yet that is exactly what happens when the media and, subsequently, people everywhere, discuss issues affecting those who are "queer." This is an umbrella term that is sometimes used to describe lesbians, gays, bisexuals, transgendered individuals, and those who are questioning their sexuality—LGBTQ, for short.

One upside to all this attention is that frank discussions can make LGBTQ lifestyles less mysterious. Human beings have a tendency to fear and dislike things that they are unfamiliar with or do not understand. The more they learn, the more willing and able they are to make proper judgments and decisions concerning an issue. One of the primary goals of this resource is to present information that brings forth a clearer understanding of what it means to be LGBTQ.

Getting Oriented

New experiences and changing circumstances often come with a period of learning and exploration called "orientation." This is a time when someone is able to become familiar with his or her surroundings and adapt to new ways of doing things. Examples of situations where orientation is a factor include starting a job or taking classes in a new school or at a different grade level. There is another definition of the word as well. Orientation also describes a long-lasting way of thinking or feeling. A person's orientation lets others know where that individual's interests lie on a given topic.

Both of these definitions of the word orientation can come into play when talking about human sexuality. Using the first definition, the new experience or changing circumstance is puberty. At this stage of development, young bodies and brains are flooded with chemicals called hormones, which make preteens and teenagers very aware of their blossoming sexuality. As they enter this new stage of their life, they go through a personal orientation process wherein they explore their sexuality and learn what best suits them as they become active sexual beings.

The other definition of the word explains itself in this context. The gender of who a person is physically and emotionally attracted to defines his or her sexual orientation.

Being Oneself

Every person, young or old, has a sense of self, which is made up of his or her actions, beliefs, and likes and dislikes, as well as the goals they set for themselves. For instance, children exhibit a sense of self by belonging to their family, the games they play, the tasks they do well, and who they want to be when they grow up. Adults define themselves by family ties as well, but their sense of self also revolves around their careers and their personal and professional accomplishments.

A person's sexuality is strongly tied to his or her sense of self. After all, human beings are sexual by nature. They want and need to make loving, physical connections with one another. There are differences in how people express their sexuality. The main difference lies in who someone is attracted to sexually. The sex (male or female) a person is attracted to defines what is called his or her sexual orientation.

A majority of people are interested in those of the opposite sex, meaning men are attracted to women, and women are attracted to men. They have a heterosexual orientation. Others have romantic and sexual feelings toward people of the same sex. They are homosexually oriented, or gay. There are still others who are attracted to both genders. These people are said to have a bisexual orientation.

In the LGBTQ spectrum, each letter (save one) represents a particular type of sexual orientation. The "L" represents lesbians, who are women who are attracted to other women. "G" stands for "gay," which is a term used to describe men who are attracted to other men. (Gay can also be used to describe both lesbians and homosexually oriented men together as a group.) Bisexual men and women, represented by the "B" in the acronym, are attracted to both sexes. Bisexuals are considered to be homosexually oriented because they deviate from the majority heterosexual orientation by also being attracted to members of the same sex. The letter "Q" stands for "questioning." Individuals may be questioning their sexual orientation or would simply rather not have a label attached to their sexual preferences.

Gender Matters

The letter "T" in LGBTQ stands for "transgender." Being transgender is not a sexual orientation. Instead, it represents a person's gender identity.

Sex is a matter of biology. It involves the chromosomal makeup of the body a person is born into, as well as a number of physical traits, notably the reproductive organs. Gender, on the other hand, deals with the way in which society expects a person to act given

According to a 2013 study conducted by the National Health Interview Survey, 96.6 percent of US adults self-identify as heterosexual. Until very recently, anyone not falling into this group was considered abnormal, even deviant.

their sex at birth. Gender identity is how a person feels inside—like a male or like a female—regardless of their sex at birth. Most people's sex and gender are in sync, meaning their gender identity matches their sex. In other words, if they have the body of a girl, they are comfortable acting like a girl, or they were born a boy and feel like a boy inside. Some people, though, are not comfortable in their own bodies. There are people who are born one sex but who identify completely—meaning physically and emotionally—with the opposite sex. These people are called transgender.

In Search of Self

Scientific studies have shown that sexual self-discovery starts early on in life. There are many examples of children exploring the boundaries of gender roles. For instance, a young boy might try on some of his mother's makeup or his sister's clothes. Likewise, young girls might do things that would prompt some to label them a "tomboy," such as playing sports and getting dirty. Experimenting in this way does not automatically mean a child identifies with the opposite gender. Aside from simply being fun, this type of exploration allows kids to ignore stereotypes and "try on" different personalities.

It is also natural for children to explore their sexuality. Most people are familiar with a game called "playing doctor," where toddlers and preschoolers get naked and "examine" each other's bodies. This is a way that young children learn about their own bodies, including their "private parts," and those of members of the opposite sex. Doctors and psychologists say that being curious and examining bodies is a normal part of a child's development, usually between the ages of three and sixteen.

Preteens and teenagers take the investigation further and begin to consider their sexuality in terms of their sexual orientation. At this point, same-sex thoughts and experiences are not uncommon, even among heterosexual teens. Thinking about or even engaging in same-sex relationships does not necessarily mean a person is

Caitlyn Jenner

In 1976, American athlete Bruce Jenner became famous for his record-breaking, gold-medal performance in the decathalon at the Montreal Olympic Games. Beginning in 2007, younger audiences came to know him as the patriarch on the hugely popular reality show *Keeping Up with the Kardashians*. These days, Jenner is famous for undergoing a transgender transformation—and she goes by the name Caitlyn.

Like it or not, Jenner has been thrust into being a role model for transgender individuals. Her transition took place later in life, when she was sixty-five. Yet she acknowledges she worries about younger trans people, especially teenagers, who face added pressures as they attempt to discover and live within their true gender identity. The best way for her to help others is to lead by example and work to change the system. As she said when she was presented with the Arthur Ashe Courage Award at the 2015 ESPY awards ceremony:

I know what my mission is. To tell my story the right way, for me. To keep learning. To do whatever I can to reshape the landscape of how trans people are viewed, how trans people are treated, and more broadly, to promote a very simple idea: accepting people for who they are.[1]

homosexually oriented. Neither does questioning one's sexual orientation or gender identity. Questioning is simply acknowledging feelings and exploring all options. However, questioning is a process many homosexual, bisexual, and transgender individuals report having gone through as they strive to find a true sense of self.

Model for Awareness

In 1989, sociologist Richard Troiden described the process by which people may come to realize and accept that they are homosexually oriented. Troiden came to his conclusions based on interviews with more than one hundred gay men. He may also have been drawing on his own experiences while growing up, as Toriden was an openly gay man. The Troiden Model of Sexual Identity[2] features four stages:

The first stage was known as sensitization. This is when a prepubescent child (one who has not yet gone through puberty) starts to have feelings that he or she may be different from others of the same gender.

In stage two, which occurs when the person is a teenager, attraction to the same sex becomes more noticeable. Thoughts about how a person should feel, like others of their gender do, are in conflict with the subject's actual feelings.

Usually beginning in the early twenties, stage three involves a greater acceptance of one's homosexual orientation. Spending time with other LGBTQ peers and learning more about LGBTQ culture help the individual feel more comfortable with their orientation.

Stage four is referred to as the commitment stage. At this point in the sexual orientation process, individuals accept the LGBTQ culture completely, as well as their own place in that culture. They are satisfied with who they are to a degree that they may be comfortable coming out to family and friends.

Accounting for Differences

Scientists, and the general public, have been trying for years to figure out why some people are LGBTQ. Sexual orientation is among

It is a perfectly natural part of development for little boys to have tea parties or for little girls to play with trucks. Such experimentation has more to do with trying out different roles and is not necessarily a clue to a person's sexuality or sexual identity.

several topics that have become part of the "nature vs. nurture" debate. This is a scientific discussion regarding the importance of biological factors, which people are born with, and personal or environmental experiences after birth on a person's behavior.

On the nature, or from birth, side of the sexual orientation debate, scientists point to studies that seem to indicate homosexual orientation has more to do with biology. Nature proponents say that sex hormones, the size and shape of the brain, and even the supposed existence of a "gay gene" are likely behind occurrences of homosexual orientation.

Other scientists hold fast to the idea that social influences and upbringing can make a person gay. The way children play and their interactions with their playmates is one factor social theorists examine. The role of parents is also important to those who believe in the power of social influences on sexual orientation. One theory that used to have a lot of support was that having a strong-minded mother and/or a weak or absent father can lead men to become gay. Sigmund Freud, the father of psychoanalysis, believed that homosexuality was a direct result of young men not being able to overcome sexual feelings for his mother—what Freud called the Oedipal complex.[3]

In a 1992 review of studies on human sexuality, Dr. June Reinisch of the Kinsey Institute at Indiana University reported finding no evidence that male sexual orientation is caused by a dominant, meaning strong and leading, mother or a weak father, or that female homosexual orientation is caused by girls choosing male role models. Nor is it true, she contended, that young people who are seduced by older, same-gender persons in their youth will become homosexually oriented. In fact, she found that under normal conditions parents have very little influence on their children's sexual orientation.[4]

Whether sexual orientation is a matter of nature, nurture, or a combination of both, our society is becoming increasingly more welcoming to LGBTQ individuals. Marriage and family are now viable options for everyone.

Reasons Unknown

Most scientists have simply refused to offer any explanation of the causes of homosexual orientation until more conclusive evidence has been presented. As Reinisch indicated in her report, scientists probably have a clearer idea about what *does not* cause most people to prefer a same-gender sexual partner. She wrote: "Children raised by gay or lesbian parents or couples are no more likely to be homosexual than are children raised by heterosexual parents."[5]

There are people in each of the nature vs. nurture camps who have stuck by their beliefs no matter what. However, it seems most likely that a combination of factors may be involved in determining sexual orientation. A pamphlet put out by the Federation of Parents and Friends of Lesbians and Gays (known today as simply PFLAG) in 1988 seems to have hit the nail on the head with this statement:

> It is believed that there are several factors which determine sexual orientation. Sexual orientation is likely to be the result of several different factors, including genetic, hormonal, and environmental. None of these factors alone are responsible for determining sexual orientation.[6]

More simply put, as the American Psychiatric Association has posted on its website, "No one knows what causes heterosexuality, homosexuality, or bisexuality."[7]

STOP HOMOPHOBIA

History of the Gay Rights Movement

The gay rights movement seeks to end any and all discrimination against LGBTQ individuals. The movement uses activism, protests, information distribution, and participation in politics and lawmaking to raise awareness of LGBTQ issues and achieve social equality. Various gay-rights groups work in concert with each other to reach the movement's goals.

Through the years, several attempts had been made to fight discrimination against the LGBTQ community. However, up until the second half of the twentieth century, there were mainly pockets of resistance against specific threats to equality. Beginning in the late 1960s, pro-LGBTQ forces created more organized campaigns and, in effect, joined forces. The result was a globally recognized movement that has remained a formidable force to this day.

Wisconsin senator Joseph McCarthy is best known for his obsession with rooting out communists in America in the 1950s. However, he was equally fervent about identifying, accusing, and intimidating homosexuals in US government positions.

Hunting for Communists and Homosexuals

A number of factors helped spark what some would call a "gay revolution" in the United States. Among them was a group made up of members of the United States government who were making life miserable for citizens they saw as a threat to the American way of life.

In 1950s, the House Un-American Activities Committee was in full swing, trying to expose alleged communist activity in the US. Communists were not the group's only target. The committee also wanted to get rid of homosexuals working for the government. Homosexuals were considered perverts and their lifestyles unnatural, and therefore they were seen as unworthy government employees.

Subcommittees were formed to look into the matter of gays holding government jobs. These groups decided that homosexuals were a possible threat to the nation. There were concerns that gays could be blackmailed into turning against the government—most likely by the feared and hated communists—in exchange for being able to keep their sexual orientation a secret.[1] As a result, efforts were begun to search for homosexuals holding government jobs and seeing to it that they were removed from their positions. In 1953, President Dwight Eisenhower made it official by issuing an executive order that stated "sexual perversion"—meaning homosexuality—was a legitimate reason for keeping someone from having a job with the federal government or outright firing them. Taking their cue from the feds, many state and local governments decided to get homosexuals out of their public offices as well.[2]

Discrimination against homosexuals in the governmental workplace made those in the LGBTQ community understandably angry. They formed groups to combat such measures and provide support for each other and their cause. The most notable among these organizations were the Mattachine Society, made up of gay men, and the lesbian-rights group the Daughters of Billitis. Their antidiscrimination efforts at first were tame and not particularly

The Mattachine Society was one of the country's first organized gay rights groups. With chapters in major US cities, the secret society's membership grew until it splintered into regional groups.

successful. Yet such groups were important because they were the foundation upon which the gay rights movement was built.

Silent No More

Among the thousands of government employees who found themselves out of a job because of antigay bias was a Harvard-educated astronomer named Frank Kameny. After his arrest for being in a spot where gay men met, Kameny was fired from his job at the Army Map Service in 1957. In addition to losing his job, he also was not allowed to apply for any government jobs for at least three years.[3]

Kameny decided to take the matter to court. After losing in federal court and the US District Court of Appeals, he argued his case in front of the US Supreme Court in 1961. His case was denied for a third and final time.

Frustrated but not defeated, Kameny decided he needed to try a new tactic. He founded and was elected president of the Washington, DC chapter of the Mattachine Society. The chapter's members started a year-long letter writing campaign in an attempt to meet with government leaders to discuss the ban on gay workers and other LBGTQ matters. A few meetings took place, but overall, not much happened to resolve the issues. Kameny then enlisted the help of the American Civil Liberties Union (ACLU), a group that works to defend and protect individual rights in the United States. ACLU lawyers helped Washington Mattachine members who had lost their jobs successfully sue John Macy, chairman of the Civil Service Commission, which was in charge of hiring and firing government employees.[4]

Kameny proved that fighting back was an option for the LGBTQ community. Increasingly, pro-gay groups, referred to as homophile groups, became activist organizations, meaning they took action against discrimination and unfair practices. Staging protests was one form of action. In 1965, homophile groups picketed in front of the White House. Aware that people thought that LGBTQ individuals were somehow wild and certainly "different," the protesters made a point to dress like everyone else, including those who were against them, did at the time. The men wore suits and ties, and the women wore dresses and high heels. They were trying to show that only their sexual orientation was different from the mainstream. They were still human beings who deserved equal rights. "We were supposed to be unthreatening," Frank Sargeant, partner of noted gay rights activist Craig Rodwell, wrote in a 2010 piece published in *The Village Voice.*[5]

Similar protests took place at other locations around Washington, as well as New York City. In Philadelphia, picketers marched in front of Independence Hall on July 4, beginning in 1965. They chose the date and location on purpose. Their goal was to remind people that LGBTQ individuals were fighting for their rights just as American revolutionaries had fought for theirs in 1776. Protesters marched silently, and as in Washington, demonstrators wore suits and dresses. The July 4 protest became an annual event and was renamed the "reminder march."

All Together Now

The protests in Washington, New York, and Philadelphia were the work of the East Coast Homophile Organizations (ECHO), which was formed in 1963. Membership in ECHO was made up of individuals from several homophile groups along the eastern coast of the United States. Chief among these were the Washington and New York City branches of the Mattachine Society; the Janus Society, a similar group based in Philadelphia; and the lesbian group Daughters of Billitis. ECHO members met monthly in a coordinated effort to combat antigay discrimination.[6]

In 1966, a number of homophile groups first came together for a national (versus the regional ECHO) pro-LGBTQ meeting called the National American Conference of Homophile Organizations, or NACHO. What started as a series of meetings became an organization that helped coordinate the efforts of many individual

Members of the Mattachine Society participated in a sip-in at a New York City bar in 1966. The society protested New York liquor laws that prevented gay customers from being served.

homophile groups across the country. NACHO supported existing homophile organizations and encouraged the formation of additional groups. Acting as a central source for information and guidance, NACHO established a legal defense fund to help members pay lawyers' salaries and other legal fees as they fought for equal rights through the court system.[7]

Unlikely Partners

Another group that influenced the formation of the gay rights movement was the mafia. This criminal organization's role was less direct than that of the congressional committees and subcommittees. At the time homosexuality was not only considered suspicious and abnormal, but it was also illegal in the United States. There were laws against homosexually oriented sexual activity, even if such acts occurred in a person's own home.

LGBTQ groups were discouraged from gathering in public places. The New York State Liquor Authority gave bars the right to refuse serving alcohol to gay customers. This order also meant that while gay bars were legal, they often could not get a license to sell alcohol from the Liquor Authority. On top of that, bars that primarily served gays were frequently raided by the police.[8]

Organized-crime bosses figured they could make a hefty profit by owning and operating gay bars. LGBTQ patrons wanted a place to gather and enjoy themselves without fear of discrimination or even arrest, and members of organized crime could make that happen. After all, they came to the job with previous experience. The mafia had made a lot of money in the US in the 1920s by smuggling liquor and running illegal drinking establishments during Prohibition— when the sale and consumption alcohol was prohibited by law.

To get around the Liquor Authority's licensing laws, the owners of gay bars declared that their establishments were private clubs, which did not need a license to sell booze. Mafia bosses paid bribes to the police so that there would be fewer raids.[9] When raids did happen, owners and customers were warned ahead of time, thanks

Sipping for Equality

In 1966, a man named Henry Hay and two other members of the Mattachine Society took it upon themselves to challenge the New York State Liquor Authority's ban on serving alcohol to gays. Inspired by sit-ins of the decade—peaceful protests where participants are seated and refuse to move until their demands are heard—Hay and company staged what they called a "sip-in."

The trio walked into a bar called Julius' in Greenwich Village, told the bartender they were gay, and requested service. The bartender refused to pour their drinks. Hay used the incident to take the matter to court, stating that the State Liquor Authority's ban was unconstitutional. The court ruled in the sip-in participants' favor, and the State Liquor Authority backed down from their stance that serving gays was punishable by law.[10]

to bribery. Being forewarned allowed gay men and women to stop dancing or touching one another and act like "responsible" customers.

Having a place in which gays, bisexuals, and transgender people could gather came at a price. The drinks were watered down and expensive, and because they were not subject to regular codes and regulations, gay bars were often rundown, dirty, and unsafe. In a way, the situation was simply another form of discrimination. LGBTQ individuals wanted better conditions and treatment not only when they went out to drink and dance, but in all areas of their lives. The anger and resentment they felt soon reached a boiling point.

Riot in Greenwich

A huge turning point in the gay rights movement can be timed almost to the instant: about 3 a.m. on Saturday, June 28, 1969. That's the time and date that the mafia-controlled gay bar called the Stonewall

Inn, located on Christopher Street in the Greenwich Village section of New York City, was raided by police.

Raids were nothing new at the Stonewall. Yet this time something unusual happened. Instead of passively accepting the raid, as in the past, the bar's two hundred or so patrons and others who had gathered outside the bar put up a fight. As police started making arrests and moving people out onto the street, a crowd of LGBTQ customers and bystanders started yelling and throwing things at the officers. Their anger was not only directed at the police, but seemingly at the grungy, mafia-owned bar as well. Lighter fluid was poured through broken front windows, and people started throwing lit matches into the bar. The raid had turned into a full-fledged riot.

The violence in and around Stonewall lasted forty-five minutes or so that evening, but the protest was not over yet. The rebellion continued for another five days, sparked by rallies attended by LBGTQ individuals and sympathetic residents of the community.

Gay Goes Radical

Immediately following the Stonewall uprising, the whole tone of the gay rights movement changed. All but gone were the days of wearing suits and dresses to fit in, and quiet or silent marches quickly became a thing of the past. The Mattachine Society tried to restore calm and order, but it was no use. In Mattachine's place came radical groups such as the Gay Liberation Front (GLF), whose slogan was "Gay Power."

Gay rights was the group's main focus. But GLF leaders considered themselves better off as part of a larger group of radical movements that had grown during the 1960s, collectively called the New Left. By banding together and supporting each other's causes, GLF leadership believed, American society could be changed for the better, for everyone.[11] Unfortunately, other movements of the New Left were not willing to join forces with GLF, some because they did not want to be linked to homosexuals. GLF had spread

On June 8, 1969, police raided the Stonewall Inn. Though raids on the gay bar were frequent, on this night the patrons fought back. The event jumpstarted the LGBTQ rights movement in the US.

itself too thin and lost its momentum. The group dissolved within a year of its formation in July 1969.

Another radical gay-rights group, the Gay Activists Alliance (GAA), had better luck. Unlike GLF, GAA focused only on gay rights. The group's methods were very "in your face"—literally. GAA was known for a protest method called "the zap." Members would confront politicians during public events and demand that they talk about their views on gay rights. Often GAA members wound up standing toe-to-toe with the objects of their protest and yelling

The First Gay Pride Parade

To commemorate the one-year anniversary of the Stonewall uprising, ECHO leaders moved the annual "reminder march" from Philadelphia to Greenwich Village. The date was also changed to June 28—the day on which the Stonewall riots occurred. In addition to serving as a reminder that the battle to defeat LGBTQ discrimination was ongoing, the march was meant to honor what many felt was a significant date in gay-rights history. The day of the march was called "Christopher Street Liberation Day," named for the street on which the now-closed Stonewall stood.

Thousands of people joined the original marchers as they moved from Greenwich Village and through midtown Manhattan, all the way to Central Park. People were heard chanting "Say it clear / Say it loud / Gay is good / Gay is proud" along the route and at the "gay-in" at the park.[12]

Every year since, additional cities have staged their own marches on or around June 28. Taking their name from the "Gay Is Proud" slogan and chant, these marches are now called Pride Parades. The marches are truly parades, with floats and bands in addition to marchers.

The Mattachine Society and the Stonewall Riots spurred the radical group Gay Liberation Front. Here, members of the group march on Times Square in 1969.

directly into their faces. The GAA also made sure they got noticed by the public and the media. Dressing up in outrageous outfits and staging events designed to antagonize those who were against gay rights were favorite tactics of the group.

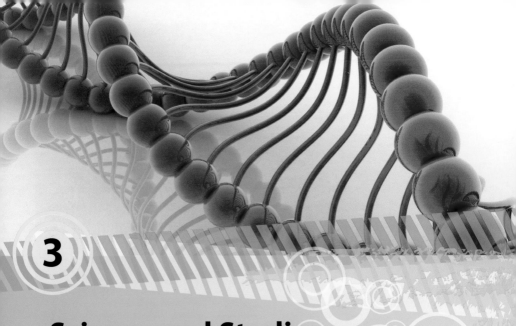

3

Science and Studies

The most basic controversy surrounding the LGBTQ community concerns the causes of homosexual orientation and gender dysphoria—the clinical term for how transgender individuals feel. The controversy arises when various groups use LGBTQ origin theories to support their beliefs. For instance, those who oppose the LGBTQ lifestyle state that sexual orientation and gender identity are learned habits that people can choose to adopt or not. Lesbians, gays, bisexuals, transgender individuals, and those who are questioning counter that no choice is involved, that people's sexual orientation or gender identity are present at birth.

In an attempt to answer questions and possibly quiet the controversy, scientists have examined sexual orientation and gender identity from nearly every possible angle. Over the years, numerous psychological, biological, genetic, and social experiments have been conducted as part of studies into gender identification and sexual behavior and attraction.

The Kinsey Report

Public discussion of homosexual orientation did not begin to surface until zoologist and sex researcher Alfred C. Kinsey published what were then startling revelations in his 1948 book titled *Sexual Behavior in the Human Male.*[1] In this study of 5,300 male volunteers, Kinsey and his associates reported that about 50 percent or one half of those surveyed had had a same-sex (homosexual) genital experience before puberty. The onset of puberty usually begins around age twelve or thirteen in males, age ten or eleven in females.

This was surprising news, especially to those who believed that the great majority of men and women were born with an exclusively heterosexual orientation. They were even more surprised to learn that, according to the Kinsey study, a full 25 percent—one in four of those interviewed—said they had had a more than incidental homosexual experience for at least three years between the ages of sixteen and fifty-five. An even larger percentage—37 percent—had had at least one homosexual experience leading to orgasm after puberty. The smallest group—10 percent—said they had been exclusively homosexual for a period of at least three years between the ages of sixteen and fifty-five.

Five years later, in 1953, Kinsey and his associates published the results of studies with females, *Sexual Behavior in the Human Female*. These results were also surprising, but they showed much less involvement in homosexual activity among women. Only 13 percent had had a homosexual experience to orgasm prior to age forty-five. Only 2 to 3 percent reported having exclusively homosexual experience.

Chicago Weighs In

The Kinsey figures for homosexual activity remained fairly constant and were the standard up until the early 1990s, when a new study,

Alfred Kinsey's groundbreaking studies on sexuality revealed much that surprised Ameircans in the 1940s and 1950s, including the prevalence of same-sex experiences.

No Mental Defect

The question of whether homosexual orientation was a mental illness was first studied in the late 1950s by Dr. Evelyn Hooker of the University of California at Los Angeles. In 1957, Hooker administered three psychological tests, including the Rorschach ink blot test, to groups of heterosexually and homosexually oriented men who were matched for age, IQ, and education levels. Based on the results of those tests, she found no differences in emotional stability and mental health between men who were homosexually oriented and those who were heterosexually oriented. However, until the early 1970s most theories about homosexuality discussed it in terms of mental disease or psychopathology. Researchers suspect that one reason for this was that psychiatrists obtained their data only from patients who had mental or emotional problems. By 1973 the American Psychiatric Association had removed homosexuality from its list of mental diseases.

"The National Health and Social Life Survey," was conducted by the National Opinion Research Center at the University of Chicago. Subjects for the Chicago study were chosen at random and were interviewed in person by 220 researchers over a period of several months in 1992. In addition to responding to the questions asked by the researchers in person, those interviewed were given written forms to complete and place in sealed envelopes. In this way, the answers they had given orally could be checked against what they wrote privately about some of the more potentially embarrassing questions.

The results of the Chicago study, based on surveys of 3,432 men and women eighteen to fifty-nine years of age, were first made public in October 1994. The study reported that only 2.8 percent of the men and 1.4 percent of the women interviewed identified themselves as homosexual or bisexual. The incidence of homosexual experience was higher, with 9 percent of the men and 5 percent of the women having had at least one homosexual experience since puberty. Almost half of those men, 40 percent of the 9 percent, had had the experience before they were eighteen but had not had one since. Most of the women were eighteen or older before they had their first homosexual experience.

Those surveyed were also asked if having sex with someone of the same gender was appealing. The idea was somewhat or very appealing to 5.5 percent of the women, while 6 percent of the men said they were attracted to other men.

The Seat of Sexual Behavior

In the 1990s, the attention of scientists investigating a possible biological link to sexual orientation turned to an area of the brain called the hypothalamus. Located at the base of the brain, the hypothalamus essentially directs a number of functions necessary for survival. Among these are energy production, sleep cycles, and the urge to have sex in order to procreate.

D.F. Swaab, a neuroscientist in the Netherlands, was the first to study the effect of the hypothalamus on sexual orientation, in 1990. After dissecting the brains of known gay men who had died, Swaab discovered that a portion of the hypothalamus was two times larger than that found in heterosexual men's brains. Around the same time as Swaab was making his discovery, researcher Laura S. Allen of the University of California at Los Angeles revealed similar findings. Allen had studied a different section of the hypothalamus than had Swaab.

Both scientists came to the same conclusion: The hypothalamuses of homosexually oriented men were noticeably different from those of heterosexual males. Furthermore, they determined that these differences in size occurred as the subjects's brains were developing in the womb, not as the result of their behavior once they became sexual aware and active. In other words, these studies

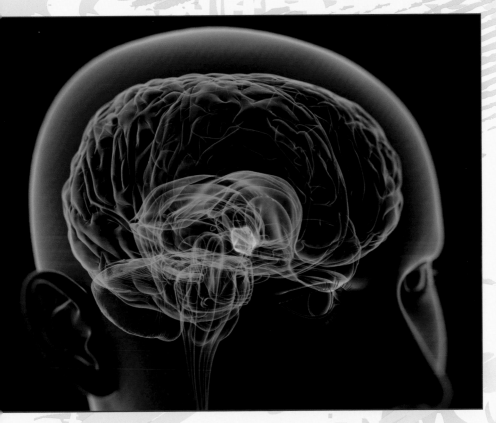

Studies have revealed that the brain might be a clue to a biological component of homosexuality. Scientists have found a size difference in hypothalamuses of heterosexual and homosexual men.

seemed to indicated that homosexually oriented individuals were born this way.[2]

In 1991, Simon LeVay examined a third portion of the hypothalamus. This time the subject brains came from men and women who had died of medical complications caused by having AIDS. The portion of the hypothalamus LeVay studied turned out to be smaller than that portion in the brains of heterosexually oriented individuals. These findings confirmed that, whether larger or smaller, the hypothalamuses of gays are "built" differently than those of their heterosexual counterparts. LeVay agreed with Swaab and Allen that the differences were the result of prenatal brain development.[3]

Scientists, including those involved in studies on the hypothalamus, admit that such research has room for error. In other words, no one can prove beyond the shadow of a doubt that being homosexually oriented is biologically predetermined. However, such studies are interesting clues leading to a possible conclusion that biology influences sexual orientation.

Gender Identity Pioneer

Dr. John Money was a psychologist and professor at Johns Hopkins University in Baltimore. A self-proclaimed "sexologist," Money conducted research into sexual perversion, or unusual sex interests and practices. However, the bulk of his work was in sexual orientation and, more specifically, gender identification.

Money is credited with bringing the terms "gender role" and "gender identity" into the vocabulary of those conducting sex research. Gender role refers to learned behaviors regarding sexual identity, meaning acting in ways that are accepted by the majority of society according to the gender a person is born. Money's classic example of learned gender roles is a woman who dresses in skirts and high heels, because that's what women in the 1950s typically wore all the time.[4] Gender identity, on the other hand, is how people feel about their sexuality in their hearts and minds, regardless of

Dr. John Money made an important distinction between gender roles (the way society expects a gender to behave) and gender identity (our personal experience of our own gender).

their biological gender at birth. His research led him to become the first scientist to recognize and explain that a person's gender identity may be in conflict with his or her physical gender.[5]

Money was considered an expert on gender matters. He wholeheartedly supported people's right to undergo surgery so that their bodies matched the gender they felt they were inside. His work also involved studying people with unusual, damaged, or missing genitalia, meaning their sex organs. Without having a clear biological gender because of their genitals, such individuals were often raised from childhood as either male or female based on a choice their parents made. Examining the lives of these subjects helped Money determine how much learned gender roles affected a person's sexual orientation and gender identity.

Money won awards for his work on gender identity. Parts of his research are still referenced today. As part of a research team, Money's research led to the founding of the Johns Hopkins Gender Identity Clinic, now known as the Johns Hopkins Sexual Behaviors Consultation Unit, in 1971. The unit specializes in human sexuality research, including gender identity concerns.[6]

Doubling Down on Research

In an attempt to determine if there is a genetic link to sexual orientation, scientists have conducted a number of studies involving twins over the past few decades. The reason is simple. Identical twins, when one egg splits in two, share the same genetic material. Two eggs fertilized at the same time results in fraternal twins, which are genetically similar and grow in the same prenatal (before birth) environment. Finding similarities between twins of either type makes it more likely that heredity has something to do with it, because of the twins' close genetic makeup.

Scientists have reasoned that if both individuals in a set of twins are gay, then genetics is at least partly involved in determining sexual orientation. The first notable study designed to test this theory occurred in 1997. Northwestern professor and psychologist John

The Case of John/Jane

Bruce Reimer and his twin brother, Brian, were born in 1965. When the brothers were seven months old, Bruce underwent an operation, called a circumcision, that went horribly wrong and damaged his penis beyond repair. Bruce's parents consulted with Dr. John Money, who recommended that Bruce undergo sexual reassignment surgery. Before his second birthday, the boy's male sex organs were removed, replaced by rough versions of female sex organs. Bruce was then raised as a girl known as Brenda.

In 1973, Money wrote in journal articles that Reimer, identified as "John/Jane" in research papers, had adapted well and readily identified as a girl. Yet nearly twenty-five years later, in 1997, researchers discovered that Reimer had never felt comfortable as a girl. In fact, at age fourteen, when he discovered the truth about his gender, Reimer decided to have surgery to become a boy again. He called himself David.[7]

The revelation embarrassed Money and called his research and his reputation into question.

Bailey and Richard Pillard, a psychiatry professor at Boston College, led the study. Bailey and Pillard studied male twins: fifty-five pairs of identical twins and another fifty-five of fraternal twins. Each pair contained one twin who was known to be homosexually oriented. Via questionnaire, they asked the brothers of each gay twin several questions about his life and sexual preferences and habits. Both brothers from the identical twin category were gay in slightly more than half (52 percent) the cases studied. Only 22 percent of the fraternal twins reported both brothers as being gay. Still, that number was significant enough that researchers saw a genetic connection in the fraternal sample as well. Findings were very similar to these when the researchers studied lesbian twins two years later.[8]

Much of what we know about gender and sexuality comes from research conducted on groups of twins. Identical twins are attractive research candidates because they share the same genetic makeup.

Another twin study, which looked at both male and female twins, took place in Australia in 2000. This time the sample size was larger, where researchers questioned a total of 4,901 sets of twins. Results of this research showed far fewer identical twins of both genders (20 percent for males, 24 percent for females) reported both siblings being gay.[9] A study out of the University of Chicago two years later revealed even lower numbers: less than 8 percent for male identical twins and approximately 5 percent for female identical twins.

Differences in results between the earlier study and research conducted in the 2000s may be tied to the way the research was gathered, including the types of questions asked and how the answers were interpreted. The ways in which subjects were found and chosen and the sample size used also could play a part.

In 2008, Swedish scientists conducted a study of 3,826 sets of twins. The overall percentages of participants who said they had at least one physical same-sex encounter during their lifetimes were 5 percent for men and 6 percent for women. The findings confirmed the results of other studies that indicated identical twins were more likely than fraternal twins to have both siblings share a homosexual orientation. However, results seemed to indicate that individual environmental factors played a more important part in a person's sexual orientation than did either genetics or the environment twins shared while in the womb.[10]

Much like the Australian and Chicago studies, the Swedish study seems to indicate that there is most likely a "gay gene." However, researchers did not exclude the possibility that biological influences such as prenatal hormones might be an inborn factor regarding sexual orientation.[11] In other words, whether nature, nurture, or some combination of the two is responsible for a person's sexual orientation is still mainly a matter of debate, one which twin studies have not been able to answer completely.

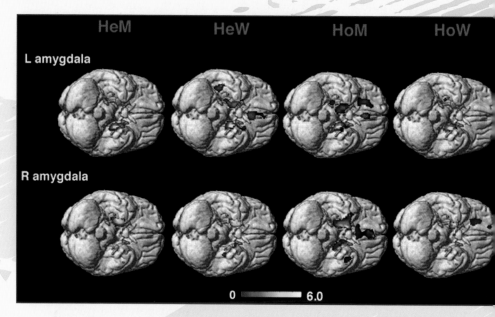

According to studies conducted by Swedish researchers, some physical attributes found in the brains of homosexual men resemble those of heterosexual women.

Back to the Brain

Also in 2008, researchers looked once again inside the human skull in an attempt to figure out if there was a connection between a person's brain and his or her sexual orientation. Instead of dissecting the brains of cadavers, however, these scientists used modern imaging technology—magnetic resonance imaging (MRI) and positron emission tomography (PET) scans—to examine the minds of the living. And whereas earlier studies had concentrated mainly on the hypothalamus, the 2008 study sought similarities in parts of the brain that had nothing to do with sexual behavior. Also examined was the structure of the whole brain.

Study participants included fifty straight men and women (twenty-five of each gender), whose brains were compared to those of forty (twenty of each gender) gay individuals. Comparing MRI results, researchers discovered that the left and right sides of the brains of gay men and straight women were roughly equal in size. The right side of the brain was larger in straight men, as it was in the lesbian brains studied as well.

PET scans of the amyglada showed cross-gender and-orientation similarities as well. The amyglada is the portion of the brain that stores memories and, of more concern to this study, processes emotions. Researchers found that gay men and straight women had a stronger connection between the amyglada and other parts of the brain dealing with emotions. Straight men and lesbians, however, showed stronger connections between the amyglada and the part of the brain that handles motor function.[12]

Reactions to the study were mixed. Some scientists felt the findings were inconclusive, meaning they left a lot of room for doubt. Others claimed that despite the similarities, there was no proof that brain size and shape had anything to do with behavior or sexual orientation. Even the study's authors admitted that additional research in this area was needed.

4

LGBTQ and Society

As recent surveys conducted by the respected Pew Research Center have shown, Americans are becoming more accepting of LGBTQ culture.[1] These days, discussions about sexual orientation and gender identity have pretty much entered the mainstream. Gay rights and concerns are getting more attention. Gay characters are featured in mainstream television shows and movies. But the situation is far from perfect.

Plenty of people, in American society and elsewhere, have very strong opinions about LGBTQ culture, both positive and negative. Some support gay rights and adopt a "live and let live" philosophy. Others believe that homosexuality and being transgender are not only somehow wrong, but immoral, and that they should be illegal. These conflicting opinions frequently clash, usually leaving LGBTQ individuals in the middle—but not helpless.

These days the LGBTQ community is openly playing a much bigger role in tackling social issues that affect them directly. Social issues are problems or areas of concern that affect a large group of people, such as a community or even an entire country. Most of the social issues surrounding LGBTQ individuals begin, and usually end, with stereotyping, prejudice, and discrimination.

Labels and Assumptions

Stereotyping means having an overly simple, general idea about how a person or group of people is supposed to think and act. Stereotypes are created when people assume and make judgments without knowing all the facts. Assumptions can be based on rumors, beliefs passed down from a person's parents, attitudes exhibited by family and friends, and even examples from media such as movies and television shows. Firsthand experience is another possibility. For example, if someone were bitten by a dog, he or she might assume that all dogs of that breed were mean and scary. Most assumptions of this type are either exaggerated versions of reality or totally untrue.

People in the LGBTQ community frequently find themselves the target of stereotyping. For instance, being effeminate, which means acting more like a woman than a man, is a major stereotype for gay men. Likewise, lesbians are stereotyped as being very tough and manly. Another popular stereotype is that gay men are flamboyant, which means they like to show off by wearing tight, flashy clothes and acting unnecessarily dramatic. Gays also supposedly are promiscuous, meaning casual in their many romantic and sexual relationships.

Stereotyping is dangerous for several reasons. While stereotypes can be used to point out positive qualities, such as labeling a particular race of people as smart or successful, they are more often negative. Most stereotyping plays up differences or accuses an individual or group of negative behavior. Also, lumping people into general categories tends to dehumanize them. In other words, it takes away their individuality and all the traits that make them unique, turning them into mere things. When people are made to seem less human, it becomes easier to treat them with indifference, or not care what happens to them.

Gay Pride and Prejudice

Stereotyping also leads to prejudice and discrimination. Prejudice is disliking or being suspicious of someone based on an unfair or stereotypical image of them. Often the word is used during discussions of race. When someone is being treated unfairly because of his or her nationality or skin color, they are said to be victims of racial prejudice. Instead of race, members of the LGBTQ community experience prejudice because of their sexual orientation.

Discrimination is prejudice in action. It involves treating people differently because of stereotypes and false impressions. Playing favorites, which is giving one person or group an unfair advantage without caring about what's right or fair, is a form of discrimination. So is failing to give someone a reward they have rightfully earned, like a pay raise or a promotion at work. Refusing to rent an apartment to a gay couple or wait on a transgender individual in a store is discriminatory as well.

There are laws in place in the United States that try to help different groups of people avoid discrimination. Only a few of these laws cover discrimination based on sexual orientation. Even fewer protect transgender individuals against gender bias, which is another word for prejudice. A 2015 report by the Williams Institute, a "think tank" within the University of California Los Angeles (UCLA) Law School, noted that thirty-two states in the US do not have antigay discrimination laws in place.

Targets for Violence

Teasing or threatening people because of their sexual orientation or gender identity is called antigay bullying. Destroying people's property, physically attacking them, or committing murder for the same reason is labeled a hate crime.

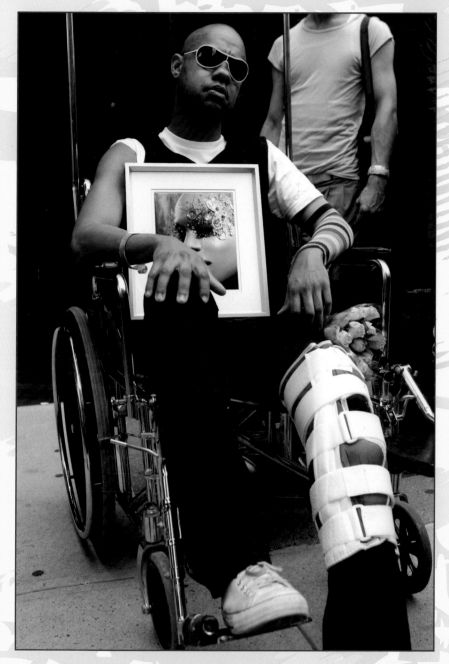

Recording artist and female impressionist Kevin Aviance was attacked by a group of men yelling anti-gay slurs in 2006. Members of the LGBTQ community are often victims of such hate crimes.

Proving It in Court

According to the National Gay and Lesbian Task Force, antigay violence is motivated by irrational fear and hatred. Even so, not every incidence of violence against LGBTQ individuals is automatically considered a "hate crime" in the United States. The federal government has stated that in order for an offense to be considered a hate crime, there must be clear-cut bias on the part of the offender. In other words, prosecutors need to show that the people committing the crime either said or did something that proved they were prejudiced against LGBTQ individuals.

Hate crimes are not at all random. Victims of hate crimes are specifically targeted for violence because of who they are, what they do, or what they believe. Such an attack on a person's identity, his or her very being, can have long-lasting psychological effects. Mental health professionals say that survivors of hate crimes are more likely to be depressed or stressed out than the victims of non-hate crimes. Adding to the problem, hate crimes usually affect more than just the intended victims. Groups of people who share the trait that triggered a hate crime also may feel afraid and unsafe, even if they didn't know the attacker or victim. Their thinking seems to be, "If it happened to that person, it could happen to me."

As reported by the Federal Bureau of Investigations (FBI) in the organization's 2013 hate crimes report, sexual orientation was the second-leading motivation for hate crimes in the United States. (The top reason was race.). The report reflects only those hate crimes that were reported. Gay rights group believe that many more violent episodes against LGBTQ individuals go unreported.

The National Coalition of Anti-Violence Programs (NCAVP) receives information regarding hate crimes against LGBTQ individuals. Each year the group puts together and publishes a report on the victims and survivors of violent crimes committed

Most major religious faiths wholly condemn or avoid actively supporting the LGBTQ community. Some places of worship, however, proudly state their acceptance of the lifestyle.

against people within this community. In 2014, the NCAVP found that nearly half of the reports they received of hate crimes against LGBTQ individuals came from gay men. Their data also showed that LGBTQ people of color and youths/young adults were among the most targeted groups that year. Gay men were more likely to encounter physical violence, while sexual violence and discrimination were most likely to affect lesbians and transgender women.[2]

Keeping the Faith

Freedom of religion is such an important concept in America. Being able to practice one's faith of choice is even guaranteed in writing in the nation's Constitution. In reality, though, taking advantage of religious freedom is not always easy for some people.

Most of the world's organized religions disapprove of homosexuality, bisexuality, and transgenderism. Many go so far as to call homosexual orientation and questioning one's gender identity sinful. Virtually every major religion points to passages in its scriptures, or sacred writings, as proof that homosexuality is unnatural and wrong. Christians use the Bible, Jews the Torah, and Muslims the Qur'an.

Very few established religions do not accept openly gay members. The majority welcome someone from the LGBTQ community, even though they strongly object to the person's sexual orientation or gender identification. However, these accepting denominations, which is what the various types of religions are called, may restrict gay participants' role in their house of worship. For instance, gays generally cannot become spiritual leaders or decision-makers.

Choosing between their faith and their sexual orientation can be painful for spiritual LGBTQ individuals. Rather than risk feeling like an outsider or not believing at all, a number of lesbians, gays, bisexuals, and transgender people have turned to more tolerant, or accepting, religions like Buddhism.

What the "Good Book" Does and Doesn't Say

According to religious fundamentalists, there are many references to homosexual behavior in the Bible, and in every instance it is condemned. As evidence of this, they point to chapters and verses in the books of Leviticus, Deuteronomy, and Genesis in the Old Testament and to Romans, Corinthians, and Timothy in the New Testament.[3]

Some religious leaders, however, do not accept a fundamentalist interpretation of the Bible as it pertains to homosexuality. In 1992, Bishop John S. Spong, formerly of the Episcopal Diocese of Newark, New Jersey, went on record as saying that even if a person was to interpret the Bible literally he or she would not be able to build an ironclad case for condemnation.[4]

Inequality in the Workplace

Fairness for LGBTQ individuals in the workplace is an issue filled with ups and downs. On the plus side, many businesses in the United States include sexual orientation in their nondiscrimination policies. As of November 2007, ninety percent of all Fortune 500 corporations—the top companies in the nation—had such policies in place. More and more companies have followed this trend as the years have gone by.

On the down side, companies that do not protect the rights of gays are not required to do so. Federal law makes sure that no American company discriminates against employees based on their race, gender, religion, nationality, or disability. That means employers cannot fire or refuse to hire and promote someone due to any of these factors. Workers who are gay, though, have no such federal guarantee. Since the early 1990s, members of Congress have tried to pass the Federal Employment Non-Discrimination Act. The bill has not yet become a law.

President Barack Obama signed an executive order protecting LGBTQ employees from workplace discrimination by the federal government on July 21, 2014. Many states offer protection as well.

According to a 2015 article in the *Washington Post*, twenty-two states and the District of Columbia have laws forbidding discrimination against gays in the workplace.[5] Also, even those companies and states that cover sexual orientation matters may not include gender identification in their antidiscrimination policies. Therefore, transgender individuals have even less job security than gay workers.

In 2014, US President Barack Obama signed an executive order barring federal contractors, meaning companies or individuals who do business with the federal government, from discriminating against anti-LGBTQ employees. Also contained in the order was a section that protects federal employees from being discriminated against because of gender identity.[6]

Health and Wellness

Everyone, regardless of their sexual orientation or gender identity, experiences health issues. However, members of the LGBTQ community seem to be more susceptible to certain medical conditions than heterosexually oriented individuals. A 2007 article in the *American Journal of Public Health* reported that lesbians are more likely to be overweight than heterosexual or bisexual women. Consequently, they also are more likely to suffer from diseases and health issues related to obesity. A survey by the journal *Tobacco Control* found that LGBTQ individuals are very likely to be smokers, while the Centers for Disease Control and Prevention has warned that gay and bisexual men, as well as transgender women, are at great risk for contracting HIV and sexually transmitted diseases.[7]

These issues are made more troublesome because of an inequality in health care coverage between the heterosexual and LGBTQ communities. The Center for American Progress has stated that LGBTQ individuals are less likely than heterosexuals to have adequate, or any, health insurance. One reason for this is because one partner in a same-sex couple is unable to be covered under his or her partner's employer-provided health-care plan. Even when they have health insurance, LGBTQ patients may not receive appropriate medical care. Doctors and other health-care professionals generally do not take special classes that address how to deal with LGBTQ patients and their particular issues. Unfortunately, discrimination can also be an issue in the health-care field.[8]

Trouble receiving and affording health care seems to be particularly difficult for transgender men and women. According to a 2011 fact sheet issued by the U.S Department of Health and Human Services, transgender people are the group most likely to be uninsured. Consequently, they do not seek medical care in a timely fashion. The fact sheet states that 88 percent of uninsured transgender people delay going to the doctor or the hospital because they cannot afford the visits. Additionally, one in five transgender men and women have been denied service from a health-care provider due to their gender.[9]

Economic Disadvantages

People of all sexual orientations and gender identities are capable of having money problems. However, research conducted by UCLA's Williams Institute indicates that a disproportionate, or unequal, number of LGBTQ individuals in the United States are poor. Institute data from 2012 showed that while approximately as many gay and bisexual men are low-income as heterosexual men, lesbians and bisexual women are poor in greater numbers than heterosexual women. It is pretty much the same story for transgender people, who were found to be four times more likely to have household incomes under ten thousand dollars than anyone in the country. Children of same-sex couples are twice as likely as children with opposite-sex parents to live in poverty.[10]

Reasons for LGBTQ poverty seem to be linked to other forms of bias. Workplace and employment discrimination seem to play a role. For instance, the fact that transgender people are twice as likely to be unemployed as members of the general population is a reason why this group's income levels are so low.[11] Families headed by

The LGBTQ community has fought for equal rights for years, including the right to equal health care. Historically, LGBTQ individuals have been denied proper care and coverage.

Transgender individuals, in particular, suffer from especially harsh discrimination in the workplace. This affects their economic status, their health, and their emotional well-being.

same-sex couples typically do not have access to the same economic advantages given to heterosexual couples. They have to pay out-of-pocket for certain benefits and programs that employers provide to families that are considered more "traditional." This might account for why twice as many children of same-sex parents are living in poverty.[12]

Special Threats to LGBTQ Teens

O ften it seems as if LGBTQ teens face even more challenges than their heterosexual counterparts. Gay, lesbian, bisexual, transgender, and questioning young adults experience the same issues as straight teens, but they also have to deal with issues surrounding their sexual orientation or gender identity. The stress of being a teenager coupled with tensions surrounding being accepted as an LGBTQ individual can be enough to lead a person into questionable, if not downright awful, decision-making that can negatively affect one's health and well-being.

There are no specific diseases or mental health concerns that are exclusive to LGBTQ teens. Yet several studies have indicated that this population does seem to suffer from certain medical and psychological conditions in greater numbers than do straight teens. Some researchers have come to the conclusion that gay teens may

Coming out is one of the pivotal moments in the life of an LGBTQ person. While it may be a terrifying prospect, it is an important step in finding acceptance from friends and family. It is also a process that helps you accept yourself.

be at greater risk for drug and alcohol abuse, sexually transmitted diseases, depression, and suicidal behavior.

Sharing One's True Identity

On the road to self-exploration, LGBTQ young people encounter a few extra obstacles as compared to their heterosexual counterparts. One of the most important of these is coming out, which means revealing their sexual orientation to those they care about and the world in general. Coming out allows people to truly acknowledge and embrace their sexual orientation, and as such, it is considered a crucial step toward self-acceptance. Many homosexuals and lesbians report suspecting or feeling that they were gay as young children, but they did not come out until years later.

Of concern for most gay teens are when to come out, who to come out to, and how to do so. There is no one correct answer to any of these concerns. The process of coming out is as unique as the individuals who go through it. Health professionals and gay support groups recommend telling people in stages, having honest conversations with one or two trusted people at a time.

Regarding when to come out, articles in the *Boston Globe* and *Newsweek* magazine have indicated that gay and transgender teens in the United States and Canada are coming out at a much earlier age than at any other time in history. As recently as the 1980s and '90s, most people came out when they were college-age or older. According to the *Globe* story, the national average age for coming out these days is around sixteen.

In spite of progress made toward achieving tolerance or acceptance of homosexual orientation, coming out can still be a perilous step for some people. Teens might find this situation particularly hard to deal with because coming out sets them apart from the heterosexual world in a way that makes them feel different, right at a time when fitting in matters most. Some individuals may find it difficult to come out because they are nervous about the reaction of others. People's attitudes toward those in the LGBTQ community can range anywhere from acceptance to hatred. Acceptance shows itself through open, honest communication and fair treatment. On the other extreme, hatred is marked by ugly threats and injustice. Therefore, LGBTQ individuals may find it necessary to seek psychological help before, during, and after the coming-out process.

Threats In Person and Online

LGBTQ teens experience their fair share of discrimination, mostly at school in the form of bullying. Bullies are people who are in a position of power. In school, students tend to be powerful because they are either physically strong or popular. Bullies use their power to harass individuals who are different from them in some way.

In the case of gay teens, the difference between them and bullies is sexual orientation or gender identity. LGBTQ teens may be targeted for bullying after they have already come out or even if a bully suspects they might be gay. Bullying is more than just being teased or picked on from time to time. Repeated verbal abuse or physical attacks, day after day, are what bullying is all about. The harassment usually starts with teasing or insults and builds from there.

Eventually, bullies may threaten their victim's safety or resort to physical violence. Bullies themselves may get hurt when their victims have had enough and decide to fight back. Serious injury and even death are the possible results of bullying, on both sides of the conflict.

Bullying is nothing new to teenagers, gay or straight. However, how bullies operate has changed over the years. Computers and the dominance of electronic communication have expanded the ways in which bullies are able to tease and harass their victims. Cyberbullying is threatening or humiliating a person using the Internet, your cell phone, or another electronic device. Text messaging, instant messaging, and posting text, photos, or videos are the tools cyberbullies use. Because online enemies can remain

Bullies often prey on LGBTQ individuals simply because they are different. Whether it is snide comments in the hallways, attacks on social media, or physical contact, it is a form of discrimination.

anonymous, cyberbullying is tough to fight or stop. Hidden identities and larger audiences for Web-based attacks make this form of bullying especially dangerous.

How often are gay teens bullied? A 2005 survey conducted across America showed that two-thirds of students in the United States who identified themselves as gay are verbally abused. Half of those kids said they also had been the victim of physical abuse because of their sexual orientation. Cyberbullying is reportedly on the rise for all kids ages ten to seventeen.

Prone to Suicide

One of the more disturbing results of the Kinsey Institute sex survey of 1978 was the finding that those with homosexual orientation, especially younger people, were far more likely to have attempted or seriously considered suicide. According to researchers Alan Bell and M.S. Weinberg, some 20 percent of gay males had attempted suicide, while another 20 percent had thought seriously about it. (Although not all of the suicide attempts or thoughts recorded in the study were related to homosexuality, about half of them were.)

In 1989, the United States Department of Health and Human Services released a study finding that gay teens were two to three times more likely to attempt to end their own lives than young adults in the general population. The report brought a great deal of attention to the subject of LGBTQ teens and suicide.

The situation has not gotten much better over time. A 2011 study found that 21.5 percent of gay and bisexual teens thought about or considered ending their own life. That number is compared to 4.2 percent of heterosexual teens who had the same thoughts and feelings.[1] Transgender teens seem to be most at risk. The National Transgender Discrimination study of 2011 reported that 41 percent of transgender teen respondents had attempted suicide at some point in their lives.[2]

Suicidal behavior includes thoughts of suicide or hurting oneself on purpose, as well as actually killing oneself. Depression and anxiety are to blame for most suicidal behavior. There's a lot for teens to be anxious about these days, including busy schedules and high expectations for performance at school and behavior at home. Mood swings caused by raging hormones don't help either. Dangerous situations in the world at large—wars, terrorism, gang violence, etc.—can sometimes bring on depression and dark thoughts.

The Centers for Disease Control and Prevention reports that suicide is the third-leading cause of death among teenagers of all orientations and gender identities. It is hard to accurately say how

The Case of Leelah Alcorn

The problem of trans teen suicide received international attention in 2014 due to the tragic death of Leelah Alcorn in Ohio. Leelah died after being hit by a tractor-trailer truck on the interstate near her home on December 28 of that year. The death was later ruled a suicide. Leelah was seventeen.

Born Josh Alcorn, Leelah had said she felt like a girl trapped in a boy's body since she was four years old. When she turned fourteen, she learned what it meant to be transgender. Her parents were devout Christians who, because of their beliefs, refused to accept Leelah's newfound identity. In a note she programmed to post on Tumblr after her death, Leelah mentioned her parents' unwillingness to accept her for who she was and feelings of loneliness as factors in her decision to end her life.

Leelah ended her note with a now-famous plea for bias against transgender people to change. It read, in part:

> The only way I will rest in peace is if one day transgender people aren't treated the way I was, they're treated like humans, with valid feelings and human rights. Gender needs to be taught about in schools, the earlier the better. My death needs to mean something. My death needs to be counted in the number of transgender people who commit suicide this year. ... Fix society. Please.[3]

many LGBTQ teens are suicidal, since most organizations don't ask about the sexual orientation of kids who hurt or try to kill themselves. However, state Youth Risk Behavior Surveys, which let kids answer anonymously and do ask about sexual orientation, suggest that gay teens are more likely to commit suicide.

Nearly one-quarter of gay and bisexual teens have considered suicide. Teens who are hiding their secret or have not been accepted by their friends and family often feel that is the only solution.

The added pressure of gay teens revealing—or hiding—their sexual orientation, plus dealing with the negative reactions of friends, family, and society, seems to be the likely reason why. Rejection by family members alone can cause a great deal of damage. Gay teens whose parents do not accept or support their sexual orientation have the riskiest behavior. As teens or later in life, they are more likely than heterosexual or accepted gay teens to get an STD, abuse drugs and alcohol, or commit suicide.

Reducing LGBTQ Teen Suicide Risk

In his 1989 report *Gay Male And Lesbian Youth Suicide*, therapist Paul Gibson wrote: "Gay and lesbian youth take tremendous risks by being open about who they are. You have to respect their courage."[4] According to Gibson, LGBTQ teens remain at high risk for suicidal feelings and behavior because of the pressures they face in conflicts with others about their homosexual orientation, especially with their peers and family.

One proposed solution to this problem is to include information and discussions about homosexual orientation in school courses that have discussions about other aspects of sexuality. Other possible solutions include programs that help teens feel accepted by their families and friends. A 2011 study conducted by Adolescent Health Initiatives at San Francisco State University's Cesar Chavez Institute indicated that LGBTQ teenagers who had experienced high rates of rejection were almost eight and a half times more likely to have attempted suicide. Researchers concluded that acceptance, by one's parents in particular, could reduce the risk of suicide and suicidal behaviors in the LGBTQ population.[5]

Substance Abuse Debate

There are lots of reasons someone might abuse drugs and alcohol. Trying to get comfort or numb the pain from fighting with one's parents of feeling lonely can lead to substance abuse. So can simply trying to fit in with other kids. These are examples of substance use

Dedicated Suicide Hotline

Talking to someone who listens and understands has been proven to keep teens from hurting themselves. Several suicide hotlines exist in the United States, but only one is designed specifically to meet the needs of gay and questioning teens. Begun in 1998, the Trevor Project operates a twenty-four-hour suicide prevention hotline and provides online support geared toward the LGBTQ community. The group's toll-free number is (866) 4-TREVOR (488-7386). Online help can be found at www.thetrevorproject.org.

due to family conflict, isolation, and fear of rejection. Gay teens are familiar with each of these situations. They find themselves at odds with family, friends, and other members of society who are uncomfortable with their sexual orientation. Feeling rejected, many gay teens turn to drugs and alcohol, which they use to try and feel better.

Experts disagree as to just how bad substance abuse issues are in the LGBTQ community. There is a famous study, conducted by the University of Pittsburgh Medical Center, that showed LGBTQ teens are 190 percent more likely to use drugs and alcohol than heterosexual teens. Some researchers and members of the LGBTQ community thought those numbers were unrealistic. They point to other studies conducted by organizations such as the Centers for Disease Control and Prevention that state LGBTQ substance abuse is more likely twice as high than abuse by straight teens. Regardless of the figures, most people believe that substance abuse is a problem for gay, bisexual, and transgender teens.

No Place to Call Home

Homelessness is a social issue that has been around for a long time. When someone does not have a fixed place to stay overnight on a regular basis, that person is considered homeless. People who live on the street or stay in shelters are considered homeless. Depending on the circumstances, homelessness can last a short time or be a long-term situation.

People lose their homes for a number of reasons. Poverty and unemployment make it impossible to pay a mortgage or rent. Substance abuse takes up so much time and money that everything else, including housing needs, becomes unimportant and gets ignored. Escaping from domestic violence can force people, usually women and children, from their homes even though they have no place else to go. People who are mentally ill often become homeless

Another method of coping that LGBTQ teens often try is substance abuse. Drinking and using drugs may numb the pain temporarily, but they will only create deeper problems.

Many LGBTQ teens are forced to run away from home because their families have rejected their lifestyle. They end up on the street or in a shelter, faced with violence and poverty.

because they are in no condition to support themselves and there are not enough facilities to care for them.

Teenagers running away from trouble at home also can wind up living on the street or in shelters. Estimates are that up to one and a half million teens are homeless in the United States at any time. Tens of thousands of those kids are gay. Many LGBTQ teens are either kicked out of their houses by their parents once their sexual orientation has been revealed. Others leave home on their own because after coming out, they feel neglected or unwanted.

Gay and straight homeless teens face many problems. Many sell themselves for sex in order to make money for food, consequently increasing their chances of getting an STD. Drug and alcohol abuse are common. Gay teens are even more at risk. Targeted by other homeless kids, LGBTQ homeless teens frequently are harassed, beaten, and robbed simply because of their sexual orientation.

LGBTQ and the Law

B ills, laws, and resolutions that directly affect the LGBTQ community are nothing new in the United States. For decades antigay groups have pushed for legislation aimed at denying, or at the very least restricting, LGBTQ freedoms. Pro-gay organizations, on the other hand, work toward getting regulations in the law books that protect their rights and end discrimination.

Battles over gay rights have been waged in the media, from the church pulpit, in the workplace, in state and federal legislative chambers, and on the streets of America. But nowhere do such arguments bring results as they do within the court system—be it a local, state, or district courtroom or even the US Supreme Court.

Long before the sexual and gay revolutions of the late 1960s and early 1970s, attempts had been made to improve the legal status of persons of homosexual orientation, but with little success. For the first six decades of the twentieth century, sexual relations between those of the same gender, referred to in legal language as homosexual acts, were illegal in every state of the Union. The laws against such acts were often labeled antisodomy laws. These acts were also illegal in many states if committed by those of heterosexual orientation.

Antisodomy laws were first enacted in the United States in the latter part of the nineteenth century, but few cases have been brought to court. Nevertheless, the people who were tried and found guilty were sometimes severely punished.[1]

By the late 1950s, however, the movement to decriminalize antisodomy laws and to permit sexual contact in private between consenting adults of homosexual orientation was gaining momentum. In 1961, the first step was taken in Illinois, where a new penal code was enacted. It declared that private homosexual acts between consenting adults were no longer a crime.[2]

Challenging Antisodomy Laws

Many attempts were made to overturn these laws, with varying degrees of success. One famous case that was taken all the way to the US Supreme Court involved the state of Georgia. The year was 1986, and the case was docketed as *Bowers* v. *Hardwick*.[3] It began with a police raid at the home of Michael Hardwick, who was found in bed with another adult male. He was immediately charged with violating a Georgia antisodomy law that criminalized any sex act involving the mouth or anus of one person and the sex organs of another. Sodomy was classified as a felony. If convicted, a person could be sentenced from one to twenty years in prison.

Hardwick filed suit in a federal district court, claiming that the Georgia law was unconstitutional. When the district court dismissed his claim without a trial, he took his case to the Circuit Court of Appeals. This time, his lawyer attached copies of a brief filed by the American Psychological Association and the American Public Health Association in a recent gay rights case in New York. By a two-to-one vote the Appeals Court held that the Georgia

Not long ago, gay couples could not be so open about their relationships. Over the years, activists have pushed for legislation protecting LGBTQ individuals, but there is still a ways to go.

statute interfered with the fundamental right of citizens to engage in private, intimate, consensual conduct.

Instead of acting on the Appeals Court's ruling, however, the state was successful in getting the US Supreme Court to review the case. The Supreme Court ruled in the state's favor, but the decision was not unanimous. In spite of the Supreme Court's 5-4 vote in favor of Georgia's antisodomy law, however, the case was never brought to trial. The state dropped all charges against Hardwick.

Unlike Georgia's antisodomy law, which applies to everyone regardless of their sexual orientation, the antisodomy law in Texas was written to apply only to those who were homosexually oriented. In 1992, six years after the US Supreme Court made its decision upholding Georgia's law, the Texas statute, titled "Sexual Conduct in Texas," was challenged by a group of professionals representing the American Psychological Association (APA), the National Association of Social Workers (NASW), and the Texas chapter of NASW.[4] The plantiffs accused the statute of being arbitrary and a violation of constitutional guarantees of equal protection under the law. They also argued that criminalizing homosexual acts does not in any way prevent or limit homosexual orientation

The district court in which the brief was filed agreed that the Texas antisodomy law was unconstitutional. That decision went to the Court of Appeals, where the district court's ruling was upheld. However, the Texas Supreme Court disagreed. Under Texas law, for a statute to be declared unconstitutional, it is not enough to show that a citizen's personal rights are harmed. It must be shown that there is harm "to a vested property right." Because property rights were not an issue in the case, the district court did not have jurisdiction and was therefore instructed to dismiss the case.

A Law Tackling Hate and Violence

Charging someone with a hate crime was a lot harder before 2009. Before then, the federal government could investigate hate crimes only if the victim was taking part in an activity that was protected

These flowers memorialize Matthew Shepard, an openly gay college student who was bound, beaten, and left to die on this fence in 1998. This tragedy advanced both state and federal hate-crime legislation. In 2009, President Obama signed into law an act named after Shepard.

under federal law, such as attending a public school. More important to the LGBTQ community, antigay bias was not included in the types of cases that would warrant a federal investigation. Prosecuting crimes against people because of their sexual orientation or gender identity were largely left to the states—and several of those did not have strong antigay laws in place.[5]

A law was passed in 2009 that gave the US federal government greater ability to investigate and prosecute hate crimes, and it provided more protection for LGBTQ individuals who were the victims of violence motivated by antigay bias. The Matthew Shepard and James Byrd Jr. Hate Crimes Prevention Act was named, in part, for a gay college student who was killed because of his sexual orientation. Matthew Shepard's murder made international headlines. Along with the dragging death of James Byrd Jr., a black man in North Carolina, the Shepard case was largely responsible for the Hate Crime Prevention Act's passage.

Antigay Legislation

There have been instances in which gay rights groups have been successful in securing protection against violence and discrimination in some cities and states. Some of these victories have later been defeated, however, by legal actions of those opposed to any tolerance or acceptance of homosexual orientation and lifestyles. One notorious instance took place in November 1992, when voters in Colorado approved Amendment 2. This amendment drastically changed the state's constitution, reversing years of efforts in all parts of the state in behalf of gay rights.[8] Amendment 2 firmly disavowed any form of protection of the rights of any citizen if based on his or her homosexual, lesbian, or bisexual orientation.

Defenders and promoters of gay rights took immediate action to stop the amendment from taking effect, and two years later their efforts were successful. By a decision of 6-1, the Colorado Supreme Court declared the amendment unconstitutional. The amendment, they declared, singled out one form of discrimination, bias against

Anderson and Grubb **v.** Branen

In 1988, the American Civil Liberties Union documented the first antigay violence case filed against the federal government: *Anderson and Grubb* v. *Branen*.[6] Marc Anderson and his companion, Jeffrey Grubb, claimed they were viciously assaulted by three agents of the U.S. Drug Enforcement Administration (DEA), Dennis Branen, Ross Kindestin, and Ed Winiefski, after a minor traffic incident. Anderson and Grubb accused the agents of abusing them verbally with a barrage of antigay epithets as well as assaulting them physically. When the police arrived on the scene, the DEA agents had Anderson and Grubb arrested and charged with various crimes.

The charges were later dropped. However, two years later, in October 1990, a civil case against the DEA agents was entered on behalf of Anderson and Grubb in federal district court in New York. The jury found that the plaintiffs had been falsely arrested and that the DEA agents used excessive force. Anderson and Grubb were awarded damages for those two counts. However, the jury found the DEA agents not guilty of arresting the pair because they were gay.[7]

homosexuals and bisexuals, and prevented them from attempting to redress any alleged wrongs against them by using the political process otherwise available to all United States citizens. As an editorial in the *New York Times* on October 14, 1994, commented, the Colorado Supreme Court's decision "brilliantly affirms the right of all citizens, whatever their lifestyle preferences, to participate in lawmaking that affects their interests." It further commented, "The right to participate equally in the political process is as old as the Union."

Pride Parade participants protest Colorado's 1992 addition of Amendment 2 to the state constitution. This amendment effectively legalized discrimination against the LGBTQ community.

"Compelling Interest"

On February 26, 2014, Arizona Governor Jan Brewer vetoed a bill giving individuals and businesses in her state the right to refuse service based on their religious beliefs. The bill, which had been passed by the Arizona legislature, was supposed to safeguard religious freedom. In other words, company owners and service providers could refuse to do business with others if doing so went against their religious beliefs. Many thought the bill was simply a way for those who oppose LGBTQ rights to get around laws making it illegal to discriminate based on sexual orientation or gender identity.

The Arizona bill stated that the state could not interfere with someone's right to practice their beliefs, in the workplace or elsewhere, unless there was a "compelling interest" for the government to do so. In other words, an individual's freedom of religion was more important unless the state could prove that the constitutional rights of society as a whole. The bill added an extra exception stating that the compelling interest had to be the best possible way to resolve the situation regarding whose rights should take precedence.

In effect following Arizona's lead, a number of other states proposed "freedom of religion" bills the following year. LGBTQ advocates believed that most if not all of these bills were a reaction to the Supreme Court ruling on a federal law allowing same-sex marriage later in 2015. Such bills were defeated in several states. The Arkansas, Utah, Michigan, North Carolina, and Indiana bills passed and became law.

Measures Banning Unhelpful Therapy

Back when being LGBTQ was considered a mental illness, some therapists believed they could "cure" homosexuals and bisexuals. The first step toward turning people away from their homosexual orientation was to begin what was known as conversion therapy. Converting, or changing, a person's attraction to same-sex

Mayors in the LGBTQ Community's Corner

For the past thirty years and more, the LGBTQ community has been able to count on the support of the United States Conference of Mayors. This nonpartisan (not for any one political party) organization of mayors from large metropolitan cities meets annually. Members of the Conference vote on proposed resolutions, then send them to political leaders in Washington. A resolution is not a law. However, by making their intentions and beliefs known, the mayors of the country's largest cities can influence policy at the state and local level.

A milestone in the gay rights movement was the 1984 resolution by the US Conference of Mayors calling for legal protection of the rights of gay males and lesbians at all levels of government. By 1986, antidiscrimination legislation or executive orders prohibiting some forms of discrimination had been passed or issued in seventy-six cities, counties, or states.

The Conference has adopted other measures and resolutions that are LGBTQ-friendly. The mayors have been part of awarding grants for HIV/AIDS prevention projects and resolved at least three times to strengthen laws protecting people from hate crimes. Also, in 2009 and again in 2014, the mayors approved a resolution in support of same-sex marriage.

individuals to opposite-sex partners was the goal of this type of therapy. Methods used in the 1950s and early 1960s could be quite harsh. Among the worst were electroshock therapy, surgical removal or mutilation of the genitals, and lobotomy, where part of the brain is removed.[9]

Conversion therapy did not completely stop once the American Psychiatric Association declared, in 1973, that homosexuality was not a mental illness. Therapy techniques in this area, however, changed. Hypnosis and plain "talk therapy" were used. Another popular method was aversion therapy, where therapists try to break a type of behavior by associating it with something negative. For example, some LGBTQ patients were given an electrical shock or drugs that made them feel ill when they looked at pictures of homosexual activity.[10]

In 1990, the American Psychological Association declared that:

> Scientific evidence does not show that conversion therapy works and that it can do more harm than good. Changing one's sexual orientation is not simply a matter of changing one's sexual behavior. It would require altering one's emotional, romantic, and sexual feelings and restructuring one's self-concept and social identity.

In the twenty-first century, conversion therapy has been deemed ineffective, as well as potentially harmful to the patient's mental and physical health. Still, a handful of psychotherapists still practice conversion therapy, as do some religious groups. In order to protect LGBTQ individuals, the state of California passed a bill that makes it illegal for licensed therapists to try to change the sexual orientation or gender identity of anyone under eighteen years of age. New Jersey and the District of Columbia passed similar bills in 2013 and 2014, respectively. Eighteen additional states introduced legislation forbidding conversion therapy on young people in 2015.[11]

Fighting for Freedom

The United States Armed Forces issued a ban on gay servicemen and servicewomen starting in 1943. The ban meant that when homosexuals were discovered in any branch of the military, they were immediately discharged, or released from duty. Members of the LGBTQ community also have been kept from joining the US Armed Forces in the first place.

Gays were excluded from military service, at least technically. According to author Randy Shilts and others, when fighting breaks out, the military needs as many recruits as possible. Branches of the armed forces can't afford to turn people away because of their sexual

Protestors in London display their disgust at the notion of a "cure" for being LGBTQ. The American Psychological Association does not support therapies aiming to change sexual orientation.

orientation. Consequently, Shilts claims, the ban hasn't always been enforced very strongly during wartime.

The LGBTQ community fought the ban for decades, calling it obvious discrimination. They have petitioned the military and the federal government to change what they consider an antigay policy. During his first presidential campaign, in 1992, Bill Clinton promised to get rid of the ban on gays in the military. He tried to do just that when he became president, but Congress refused to agree to the plan. In 1993, President Clinton signed into law a compromise policy concerning gays in the military. Nicknamed "Don't Ask, Don't Tell," the new law meant military recruiters could not ask if someone is gay, and gay servicemen and servicewomen were to keep their sexuality a secret.

Like Bill Clinton before him, Barack Obama pledged as part of his campaign in 2008 to change how the armed forces operate and make them open to everyone. In 2010, during his first term in office, President Obama made good on his promise and began the process of repealing "Don't Ask, Don't Tell." In May of that year, the US Congress voted to repeal the policy, subject to a review by the Pentagon. On December 22, President Obama signed a bill that had passed in both the House and the Senate, that repealed the policy. The bill could not become law, however, until sixty days after the Pentagon's report was approved and the Defense Department had new rules and regulations in place that supported the law. It took almost nine months, but eventually all those requirements were met. On September 20, 2011, "Don't Ask, Don't Tell" was officially history.

Additional policy changes in 2013 gave same-sex couples access to several military benefits that heterosexual members of the U.S Armed Forces and their families had enjoyed for years. Among these benefits were military identification cards for same-sex partners of military personnel, access to child care and youth programs, and sexual assault counseling. Not included at that time were housing and medical and dental benefits. Those and a few other benefits were reserved for married couples, and at that time same-sex marriage was not covered under federal law.[12]

On June 9, 2015, the US Department of Defense changed how the armed forces protect LGBTQ troops from discrimination and bias. Defense Secretary Ash Carter announced that discrimination claims made by gay, lesbian, bisexual, and transgender service members would be are investigated and addressed by the Military Equal Opportunity program office, which handles all other military discrimination complaints. Prior to "Don't Ask, Don't Tell" being rescinded and other policy changes being made, LGBTQ troops filed discrimination complaints with the Defense Department's Office of the Inspector General.[13]

Joined in Matrimony

By 2010, Canada was one of six countries that recognized same-sex marriage on a national level. The Canadian Parliament passed the Civil Marriage Act in 2005. Before then, the question of whether same-sex marriage should be legal was left to individual provinces. Eight of the ten Canadian provinces had approved such marriages by the time the new federal law came into effect.

In the US around that time, individual states determined for themselves whether same-sex marriage was legal. Generally, the federal government did not get involved in such matters. In fact, the Defense of Marriage Act of 1996 (DOMA) prohibited federal recognition of state-approved same-sex marriages. In other words, the government did not give federal benefits, such as pensions and health benefits, to gay couples married in a state that allowed same-sex marriage. Also, states did not need to acknowledge that a same-sex couple was married under the laws of another state. Many of the forty-five states that had deliberately banned same-sex marriage by law supposedly patterned their legislation after DOMA.

The situation took a turn beginning in 2013. That year, in *United States* v. *Windsor*, the US Supreme Court ruled that a section of DOMA, which specified that marriage was only between one

Supporters of marriage equality gathered on the steps of the US Supreme Court to celebrate after the court ruled that bans on same-sex marriage were unconstitutional.

man and one woman in the eyes of the federal government, was unconstitutional.[14] The ruling meant that same-sex couples could claim federal benefits in states where same-sex marriage was legal. In other words, the federal government would recognize same-sex marriages as long as they were performed in a state where such unions were legal.

In April 2015, the Supreme Court heard arguments in *Obergefell v. Hodges*, an appeals case concerning the right of same-sex spouses to claim certain federal benefits even if they lived in states where same-sex marriage was illegal. On June 26 of that year the Supreme Court ruled that state bans on same-sex marriage were unconstitutional. Officially, same-sex marriage had become legal nationwide.

Information and Support

For a long time now, LGBTQ individuals have found that banding together and supporting each other is a good way to stay strong and get things done. Early groups such as the Mattachine Society and Daughters of Billitis gave gays and lesbians a voice and let LGBTQ individuals know they were not alone. The gay rights movement saw the amplification of that voice through the work of peaceful and radical advocacy organizations. These days LGBTQ organizations include advocacy groups and support networks that offer social and even professional networking opportunities.

The LGBTQ community in the United States also is aware that one important key to gaining understanding and acceptance from antigay forces is knowledge. That comes through gathering and sharing information. LGBTQ organizations frequently provide information on sexual orientation and gender identity, as well as gay-related news and event announcements.

Lending a Hand

All teens could use someone who believes in them and has their back. For LGBTQ teens, however, that kind of support can be hard to come by. Traditional sources of support may be weak or nonexistent. For instance, family members and friends might be too upset or weirded out by same-sex orientation to be of much help. Teachers and school counselors are not always well equipped to handle bullying and other gay concerns. And misunderstandings about what it means to be LGBTQ might keep some clergy members from offering useful assistance.

That's why gay teens often turn to advocacy groups for help and encouragement. In general, organizations are formed when someone sees a need that isn't being met and wants to fill the gap. Others are created when a person wants to share his or her experiences, in the hope that doing so will help others in a similar situation make wise choices. Many LGBTQ support groups and programs in the United States exist because of both these reasons.

There are groups that offer support for nearly every LGBTQ issue imaginable. Some address feeling safe and being treated fairly at school. Some concentrate on religious differences or legal concerns associated with sexual orientation. Still others tackle health and wellness issues in the LGBTQ community. Best of all, there are organizations that offer gay teens the chance to talk about what's going on in their lives, good or bad, and just be themselves.

At the local level are LGBTQ community centers. These are gathering places designed to meet the social, cultural, recreational, health, and political advocacy needs of gay men and women. Depending on what programs are offered, center members can watch movies, hear guest speakers, receive health care or counseling, organize events, or simply hang out with people who have the same sexual orientation. Some of these centers are geared toward specific gay groups, such as teenagers and young adults. CenterLink, the organization that supports LGBTQ community centers in the US and abroad, can help you find a center in your area. The group's website is http://www.lgbtcenters.org.

Obviously, national organizations serve a greater number of people than local community centers. Education and advocacy, which is raising awareness and working together for a common cause, are the main focus of national support groups. Two American organizations that have been around a while and have excellent reputations are Parents, Families and Friends of Lesbians and Gays, and the Gay Lesbian Straight Education Network.

Waving the PFLAG of Support

Parents, Families and Friends of Lesbians and Gays (PFLAG) began after one parent said enough is enough. In 1972, Jeanne Manford took part in a gay pride march with her son, carrying a sign that read, "Parents of Gays: Unite in Support for Our Children." Response to the sign was so overwhelmingly positive that Manford decided to start a support group that would bring parents and their LGBTQ children closer together. The first meeting of what was then called Parents FLAG was held in a church and attended by about twenty people.[1]

Since then, PFLAG has grown quite a bit. More than five hundred chapters are located across the country, in all fifty states. The organization serves hundreds of thousands of members. As the group's name says, PFLAG offers support to the parents, family, and friends of gay people but also works with LGBTQ individuals themselves. Education and advocacy efforts cover gay rights issues in the home, workplace, school, and military. PFLAG even has a Families of Color Network, which discusses issues of race and diversity within the LGBTQ community.

Contacting or joining PFLAG is easy. The group's website, at http://community.pflag.org, has lots of information to get you started. A search feature helps you find a chapter in your area.

Members of PFLAG show their support during St. Louis's PrideFest parade. PFLAG has more than five hundred chapters in the US.

Join the Network

The Gay Lesbian Straight Education Network (GLSEN) is a national organization that works to create a safe and supportive environment for all students at school. GLSEN was created by a group of gay and lesbian teachers in 1995. As educators, they felt there was a lack of resources available for LGBTQ support in the nation's schools. They also were looking for ways to bring discussions of gay issues into the classroom.[2]

Rather than being simply pro-gay, GLSEN welcomes gay and straight members of all races, faiths, and backgrounds. Greater diversity, or variety, through respect and understanding is the group's goal. Toward that end, the organization also works with schools around the country to fight discrimination based on race and gender, as well as sexual identity.

There are forty GLSEN chapters nationwide. Each chapter offers teachers, students, and outside supporters a set of tools to help them strengthen diversity in their schools and communities. The organization runs several programs that raise awareness of bullying and harassment. Working with legislators, GLSEN also tries to pass laws that stop discrimination and make schools safer for everyone.

How to Build a Gay-Straight Alliance

GLSEN also supports and registers gay-straight alliances (GSAs). As you can tell by the name, these student-run clubs have members who are gay and straight. GSAs are formed to improve the quality of life for students at school, regardless of sexual orientation or gender identity. Like any other club, they hold regular meetings and host events that call attention to their cause.

GSAs can be found in many parts of the world. The United States, which is where the idea of GSAs began, has more of these organizations than any other country. More than four thousand GSAs are registered with the central office of GLSEN.

To start your own GSA, follow whatever rules your school has for creating clubs and student organizations. Usually you have to ask

This image from the fortieth celebration of Washington, DC's Capital Pride Parade shows how diverse LGBTQ support is today. The LGBTQ lifestyle has become increasingly acceptable to Americans.

Speaking Out Through Silence

One of GLSEN's most well-known programs is Day of Silence, which is a peaceful way to protest the harassment and discrimination of LGBTQ students on school campuses nationwide. For one day each year, students in middle schools, high schools, and colleges in the United States do not speak. Their silence represents the way LGBTQ students are pressured into remaining quiet about their lives and issues that concern them. Other programs under GLSEN's "Days of Action" series include No Name Calling Week, Ally Week, and TransAction!, which is a day set aside to discuss gender roles and identity. Learn more at http://www.glsen.org

permission and write a proposal. The proposal outlines what kind of group you're forming, how often you plan to meet, what the group's goals are, and a few ways in which those goals will be met.

As a faculty advisor, which all student groups must have, pick someone who has shown sensitivity toward all students, regardless of sexual orientation. The advisor helps guide the group and works closely with the school's administration to get things done. He or she needs to be someone you can trust and who believes in your cause.

Next, you need to get the word out about your GSA. Some kids may want to join your group but are worried about what other people will think of their participation. You may want to hold meetings off school grounds, at least at first. This will help nervous possible members feel more comfortable about joining.

Two, Four, Six, Eight . . . Communicate!

The mission of the Gay and Lesbian Alliance Against Defamation (GLAAD) is to make sure the LGBTQ community is represented fairly, meaning without bias, in the media.[3] The organization manages this by working with the English- and Spanish-language

Members of Travella High School's Gay-Straight Alliance in Coral Gables, Florida, pose for their yearbook photo. If your school doesn't have a GSA, think about starting one.

news media, suggesting stories reporters might want to cover and pointing out information they believe is incorrect in stories that have already been released. GLAAD also tries to work within the entertainment business to include LGBTQ characters that are positive role models in television shows and movies.

Another GLAAD project is offering communications assistance to advocacy groups. The organization also attempts to make sure that the effects of GLAAD's work can be felt on social media sites.

Getting Better All the Time

Upset because there were so many LGBTQ teen suicides, author Dan Savage was moved to action. Savage and his then partner (now husband), Terry Miller, formed what has become known as the It Gets Better Project, a worldwide movement helping LGBTQ children and young adults confront harassment and bullying. The project shares stories of hope and encouragement with LGBTQ teens in video and written formats. Messages, which all revolve around the theme "It Gets Better," are recorded by LGBTQ and straight teens, adults, friends, family, and celebrities.[4]

Since it began in 2010, the It Gets Better Project has lived up to its name and gotten better. In addition to words of encouragement, the project currently offers suicide prevention resources, legal-education referrals, and video and graphic content available to media and social networking outlets.

Supporting Yourself

Feeling accepted is a crucial part of self-esteem, which is how valuable and capable a person thinks he or she is. Without acceptance, a person's confidence can be badly shaken. Mental health professionals suggest that people who have trouble with self-esteem, no matter their age or sexual orientation, first find a way to accept themselves for who they are. Basically, the trick is to be kind to yourself. Replace any negative thoughts or self-doubts with positive reinforcement. Pay more attention to everything that makes

Dan Savage (left) and husband Terry Miller (right) started the It Gets Better Project in 2010 in the hopes of helping prevent suicide among LGBTQ youth.

you a good person than you do to the negativity thrown at you by outside forces.

Taking steps toward building self-esteem isn't going to affect what other people say and do. Yet coming to terms with who you are, and being comfortable with and proud of that person, will help you deal when life gets harsh. More importantly, a strong, healthy sense of self will help you enjoy all the good that comes your way.

Chapter Notes

Chapter 1: Orientation and Identification

1. Mia Lardiere, "9 Times Caitlyn Jenner 'Got it Right' As an LGBT Role Model So Far," Celebuzz, July 23, 2015, http://www.celebuzz.com/2015-07-23/9-times-caitlyn-jenner-got-it-right-as-an-lgbt-role-model-so-far/ (retrieved July 2015).

2. Joan Littlefield Cook and Greg Cook, "The Development of Sexual Orientation," *Child Development: Principles and Perspectives*, May 2014, http://www.education.com/reference/article/development-sexual-orientation/ (retrieved July 2015).

3. Ryan D. Johnson, "Homosexually: Nature or Nurture," AllPsych, April 2003, http://allpsych.com/journal/homosexuality/#.VbVhS_lczD- (retrieved July 2015).

4. June Machover Reinisch, ed., *Masculinity/Femininity: Basic Perspectives* (New York: Oxford University Press, 1987), p. 8–9.

5. Ibid.

6. Tineke Bodde, "Why Is My Child Gay?", Federation of Parents and Friends of Lesbians and Gays, Inc., 1988.

7. Staff, "LGBT—Sexual Orientation," American Psychiatric Association, http://www.psychiatry.org/lgbt-sexual-orientation (retrieved July 2015).

Chapter 2: History of the Gay Rights Movement

1. Stephanie Watson, *Gay Rights Movement* (Minneapolis, MN: ABDO Publishing Company, 2014), p. 28-9

2. Linas Alsenas, *Gay America: Struggle for Freedom* (New York, NY: Amulet Books, 2008), p. 59.

3. Watson, *Gay Rights Movement*, p. 39.

4. Ibid, p. 42-43.

5. Fred Sargeant, "1970: A First-Person Account of the First Gay Pride March," *The Village Voice*, June 2010, http://www.villagevoice.com/news/1970-a-first-person-account-of-the-first-gay-pride-march-6429338 (retrieved August 2015).

6. Staff, "Homophile Movement, U.S.," GLBTQ.com, http://www.glbtq.com/social-sciences/homophile_movement,3.html (retrieved August 2015).

7. Staff, " Finding Aid to the North American Conference of Homophile Organizations Records, 1966-1970 Coll2011.065," Online Archive of California, http://www.oac.cdlib.org/findaid/ark:/13030/c8d21vz6/ (retrieved August 2015).

8. PBS Staff, "Why Did the Mafia Own the Bar?", *American Experience: Stonewall Uprising*, http://www.pbs.org/wgbh/americanexperience/features/general-article/stonewall-mafia/ (retrieved July 2015).

9. Scott Simon, "Remembering a 1966 'Sip-in' for Gay Rights," NPR Weekend Edition, June 2008, http://www.npr.org/templates/story/story.php?storyId=91993823 (retrieved July 2015).

10. Simon,"Remembering a 1966 'Sip-in' for Gay Rights."

11. Alsenas, *Gay America: Struggle for Freedom.*

12. Bianca Wythe, "How the Pride Parade Became Tradition," Inside American Experience, June 2011, http://www.pbs.org/wgbh/americanexperience/blog/2011/06/09/pride-parade/ (retrieved August 2015).

Chapter 3: Science and Studies

1. The Kinsey Institute, "Prevelance of Homosexuality: The 1948 and 1953 Studies of Alfred Kinsey," Kinsey Institute Bibliography, http://www.kinseyinstitute.org/resources/bib-homoprev.html (retrieved August 2015).

2. Ryan D. Johnson, "Homosexually: Nature or Nurture,"

AllPsych, April 2003, http://allpsych.com/journal/homosexuality/#.VbVhS_lczD- (retrieved July 2015).

3. Ibid.

4. Staff, "John Money (1921-2006)," GoodTherapy.org, http://www.goodtherapy.org/famous-psychologists/john-money.html (retrieved August 2015).

5. Benedict Carey, "John William Money, 84, Sexual Identity Researcher, Dies," *New York Times,* July 2006, http://www.nytimes.com/2006/07/11/us/11money.html?_r=0 (retrieved August 2015).

6. Psychiatry and Behavioral Sciences staff, "Sexual Behavior Consultation Unit," Johns Hopkins Medicine, http://www.hopkinsmedicine.org/psychiatry/specialty_areas/sexual_behaviors/ (retrieved August 2015).

7. Carey, "John William Money, 84, Sexual Identity Researcher, Dies."

8. Deborah Blum, *Sex on the Brain: The Biological Differences Between Men and Women* (New York, NY: Penguin Books, 1997), p. 132-33.

9. JM Bailey, et al."Genetic and environmental influences on sexual orientation and its correlates in an Australian twin sample," *Journal of Personality and Social Psychology* 8, no. 3 (March 2000): p. 524–36.

10. Niklas Langström, et al., "Genetic and environmental effects on same-sex sexual behavior: a population study of twins in Sweden" (abstract), February 2010, http://www.ncbi.nlm.nih.gov/pubmed/18536986 (retrieved August 2015).

11. Michael Balter, "Gay Is Not All In the Genes," News from *Science Magazine,* June 2008, http://news.sciencemag.org/brain-behavior/2008/06/gay-not-all-genes (retrieved August 2015).

12. Rob Stein, "Brain Study Shows Differences Between

Gays, Straights," *Washington Post,* June 2008, http://www.washingtonpost.com/wp-dyn/content/article/2008/06/22/AR2008062201994.html (retrieved August 2015).

Chapter 4: LGBTQ and Society

1. Bruce Drake, "How LGBT adults see society and how the public sees them," Pew Research Center, http://www.pewresearch.org/fact-tank/2013/06/25/how-lgbt-adults-see-society-and-how-the-public-sees-them/ (retrieved August 2015).

2. Osman Ahmed and Chai Jindasurat, "Lesbian, Gay, Bisexual, Transgender Queer, and HIV-Affected Hate Violence in 2014," The National Coalition of Anti-Violence Programs, http://www.avp.org/storage/documents/Reports/2014_HV_Report-Final.pdf (retrieved August 2015).

3. Stanton L. Jones, "The Loving Opposition," *Christianity Today,* July 19, 1993, p. 20–25.

4. Episcopal Bishop John S. Spong, *Is Homosexuality A Sin?* (Washington, DC: Federation of Parents and Friends of Lesbians and Gays, Inc., 1992), p. 11–12.

5. Lydia DePillis, "This is the next front in the battle for gay rights," *Washington Post,* June 2015, http://www.washingtonpost.com/news/wonkblog/wp/2015/06/26/this-is-the-next-frontier-in-the-battle-for-gay-rights/ (retrieved August 2015).

6. Mark Joseph Stern, "Obama Signs Historic LGBT Non-Discrimination Order," *Slate,* July 2014, http://www.slate.com/blogs/outward/2014/07/21/obama_signs_history_executive_enda_forbidding_lgbt_discrimination.html (retrieved August 2015).

7. Sean Cahill and Kellan Baker, "The Case for Designating LGBT People as a Medically Underserved Population and as

a Health Professional Shortage Area Population Group," The Fenway Institute, August 2014, http://thefenwayinstitute. org/wp-content/uploads/MUP_HPSA-Brief_v11- FINAL-081914.pdf (retrieved August 2015).

8. Laura E. Durso, et al., "LGBT Communities and the Affordable Care Act," Center for American Progress, October 2013, https://www.americanprogress.org/wp-content/ uploads/2013/10/LGBT-ACAsurvey-brief1.pdf (retrieved August 2015).

9. Staff, "Lesbian, Gay, Bisexual, and Transgender Populations: Selected Findings from the 2011 National Healthcare Quality and Disparities Report," http://archive.ahrq.gov/research/ findings/nhqrdr/nhqrdr11/lgbt.html (retrieved August 2015).

10. Brad Sears and Lee Badgett, "Beyond Stereotypes: Poverty in the LGBT Community," The Williams Institute, June 2012, http://williamsinstitute.law.ucla.edu/headlines/beyond- stereotypes-poverty-in-the-lgbt-community (retrieved August 2015).

11. Staff, "Just the Facts: LGBT Data Overview 2015," The Williams Institue, May 2015, http://williamsinstitute. law.ucla.edu/datablog/just-the-facts-data-overview_2015 (retrieved August 2015).

12. Sears and Badgett, "Beyond Stereotypes: Poverty in the LGBT Community."

Chapter 5: Special Threats to LGBTQ Teens

1. Kathleen Gilbert, "Study: gay teens five times more likely to attempt suicide," LifeSite News, April 2011, https://www. lifesitenews.com/news/study-gay-teens-five-times-more- likely-to-attempt-suicide (retrieved August 2015).

2. Hugh Ryan, "There's a Suicide Problem Among Transgender Youths—and We Need to Help," TakePart.com, May 2015,

http://www.takepart.com/article/2015/05/15/transgender-mental-health-services (retrieved August 2015).

3. "An Ohio transgender teen's suicide, a mother's anguish," CNN Online, January 2015, http://www.cnn.com/2014/12/31/us/ohio-transgender-teen-suicide/index.html (retrieved August 2015).

4. Paul Gibson, "Gay Male And Lesbian Youth Suicide," US Department of Health and Human Service's *Report of the Secretary's Task Force on Youth Suicide*, 1989, volume 3, http://www.qrd.org/qrd/www/orgs/avproject/youth_suicide.htm (retrieved August 2015).

5. Joseph Shapiro, "Study: Tolerance Can Lower Gay Kids' Suicide Risk," NPR, December 2008, http://www.npr.org/templates/story/story.php?storyId=98782569 (retrieved August 2015).

Chapter 6: LGBTQ and the Law

1. David F. Greenberg, *The Construction of Homosexuality* (Chicago: University of Chicago Press, 1988), p. 455–456.

2. Ibid.

3. *Bowers v. Hardwick*, American Psychological Association Amicus Curiae Briefs, "Further Lesbian and Gay Male Civil Rights," (September 1991), p. 952–953.

4. *The State of Texas* v. *Linda Morales, Tom Doyal, Patricia Cramer, Charlotte Taft, and John Thomas*, Brief for Amici Curiae, American Psychological Association, National Association of Social Workers, and Texas Chapter of the National Association of Social Workers (December 14, 1992).

5. Staff, "Matthew Shepard and James Byrd, Jr. Hate Crimes Prevention Act: What You Need to Know," Anti-Defamation League, http://www.adl.org/assets/pdf/combating-hate/

What-you-need-to-know-about-HCPA.pdf (retrieved August 2015).

6. *Anderson and Grubb* v. *Branen*, American Civil Liberties Union, Lesbian and Gay Rights Project, Docket 1993, p. 3.

7. "Gay-bashing victims overcome prejudice to win civil settlements," The Free Library, American Association for Justice, http://www.thefreelibrary.com/Gaybashing+victims+overcome+prejudice+to+win+civil+settlements.-a053913323 (retrieved August 2015).

8. *Colorado*, American Civil Liberties Union, Lesbian and Gay Rights Project, Docket 1993, p. 12.

9. Lila Shapiro, "Straight Talk: How Mathew Shurka And His Conversion Therapist Renounced The 'Gay Cure," *Huffington Post*, June 2013, http://www.huffingtonpost.com/2013/06/25/mathew-shurka-conversion-therapy_n_3466943.html (retrieved August 2015).

10. Tia Ghose, "Why Conversion Therapy Is Harmful," LiveScience.com, April 2015, http://www.livescience.com/50453-why-gay-conversion-therapy-harmful.html (retrieved August 2015).

11. Lori Grisham, "What you need to know about 'conversion therapy,'" *USA Today*, April 2015, http://www.usatoday.com/story/news/nation-now/2015/04/10/conversion-reparative-sexual-reorientation-therapy/25515619/ (retrieved August 2015).

12. Karen Parrish, "Same-Sex Couples Can Claim New Benefits by October," US Department of Defense news, February 2013, http://www.defense.gov/News/NewsArticle.aspx?ID=119260 (retrieved August 2015).

13. Tom Vanden Brook, "Pentagon protects gay troops," *USA Today (Rochester Democrat and Chronicle)*, Section B, p. 1, Wednesday, June 10, 2015.

14. Dylan Matthews, "The Supreme Court struck down part of DOMA. Here's what you need to know," *Washington Post*, June 2013, http://www.washingtonpost.com/news/wonkblog/ wp/2013/06/26/the-supreme-court-struck-down-doma- heres-what-you-need-to-know/ (retrieved August 2015).

Chapter 7: Information and Support

1. Staff, "PFLAG's History," PFLAG, http://community.pflag. org/page.aspx?pid=267 (retrieved August 2015).
2. Staff, "Who We Are," GLSEN, http://www.glsen.org/learn/ about-glsen (retrieved August 2015).
3. Staff, "About GLAAD," GLAAD, http://www.glaad.org/about (retrieved August 2015).
4. Staff, "What is the It Gets Better Project?," It Gets Better Project, http://www.itgetsbetter.org/pages/about-it-gets- better-project/ (retrieved August 2015).

Glossary

access—A way of getting to something.

advocacy—The act of supporting a cause or set of beliefs.

assault—To commit violence against someone.

ban—Officially keeping people from doing something.

bias—The belief that someone or something is better than others

bisexual—A type of sexual orientation in which a person is romantically and sexually attracted to people of both sexes.

conversion—Changing from one type to another.

defamation—The act of saying something that is not true in order to make others think negatively about someone or something.

discrimination—Treating a group of people unfairly because they are different, or seem to be different, from the majority.

orientation—A person's feelings or beliefs that dictate how he or she lives life.

petition—To strongly ask for or demand something, usually in writing.

seduce—To convince someone to have sex.

sensitization—The act of making people more aware of something.

stereotyping—Incorrectly and unfairly believing that all members of a group are the same.

transgender—Describes a person whose sexual identity does not match up with his or her sex at birth.

For More Information

Canadian Lesbian and Gay Archives
50 Charles Street East
Toronto, ON M4Y 2N6
(416) 777-2755
Website: http://www.clga.ca/
The CLGA collects and maintains information related to gay
and lesbian life in Canada and elsewhere. The organization
makes its books and articles, artifacts, audio and video
recordings, and artwork available to the public for education and
research.

The Gay, Lesbian and Straight Education Network
90 Broad Street, 2nd Floor
New York, NY 10004
(212) 727-0135
Website: http://www.glsen.org
The Gay, Lesbian and Straight Education Network works with
educators, policy makers, community leaders, and students to
protect students from bullying and harassment and secure safe
school laws and policies.

The Human Rights Campaign
1640 Rhode Island Avenue NW
Washington, DC 20036-3278
(800) 777-4723
Website: http://www.hrc.org
Founded in 1980, the Human Rights Campaign (HRC) is
a national lesbian, gay, bisexual, and transgender civil rights
organization. HRC advocates on behalf of LGBTQ Americans,
mobilizes grassroots actions in diverse communities, invests
strategically to elect fair-minded individuals to office, and
educates the public about LGBTQ issues.

The National Gay and Lesbian Task Force
1325 Massachusetts Avenue NW, Suite 600
Washington, DC 20005
(202) 393-5177
Website: http://www.thetaskforce.org/
With several chapters across the United States, the National
Gay and Lesbian Task Force supports the LGBTQ community
by training activists, organizing campaigns to promote pro-gay
legislation, and providing research and policy analysis.

National Youth Advocacy Coalition
1638 R Street, NW, Suite 300
Washington, DC, 20009
(800) 541-6922
Website: http://www.nyacyouth.org
The National Youth Advocacy Coalition is a social justice
organization that offers advocacy and youth engagement in an
effort to end discrimination against LGBTQ teens.

Parents and Friends of Lesbians and Gays (PFLAG)
1726 M Street NW, Suite 400
Washington, DC 20036
(202) 467-8180
Website: http://community.pflag.org/
PFLAG promotes the health and well-being of gay, lesbian,
bisexual and transgender people, their families, and friends
through support, education, and advocacy.

PFLAG Canada
1633 Mountain Road, Box 29211
Moncton, NB E1G 4R3
Canada
Website: http://www.pflagcanada.ca
PFLAG Canada provides informtion and support to LGBTQ
teens and adults, as well as their friends and loved ones.

Further Reading

Andrews, Arin. *Some Assembly Required*. New York: Simon and Schuster, 2014.

Bausum, Ann. *Stonewall: Breaking Out in the Fight for Gay Rights*. New York: Viking Books, 2015.

Gottfried Hollander, Barbara. *Marriage Rights and Gay Rights: Interpreting the Constitution*. New York: Rosen, 2015.

Huegel, Kelly. *GLBTQ: The Survival Guide for Gay, Lesbian, Bisexual, Transgender, and Questioning Teens*. Minneapolis, MN: Free Spirit Publishing, Inc., 2011.

Marcovitz, Hal. *Teens & LGBT Issues*. Broomhall, PA: Mason Crest, 2014.

Moon, Sarah, and James Lecesne, eds. *The Letter Q: Queer Writers' Letters to Their Younger Selves*. New York: Scholastic Books, 2014.

Savage, Dan, and Terry Miller, eds. *It Gets Better*. New York: Penguin Books, 2012.

Ambiente Joven (Spanish language)
www.ambientejoven.org/

The Cool Page for Queer Teens
www.bidstrup.com/cool.htm

GayCanada
www.cglbrd.com/

In The Mix: Gay Teens
www.pbs.org/inthemix/shows/show_whatsnormal_
gayteens.html

Youth Resource
www.youthresource.com/

Index